LETTERS FROM BUD

The WW2 War Diary and Letters of John "Bud" Brandenburg

Edited and With Historical Notes by
Molly Brandenburg

Happy Publishing

LETTERS FROM BUD: *The WW2 Letters and War Diary of John "Bud" Brandenburg*

Copyright © 2019 Molly Brandenburg

ISBN 978-1-64467-028-6

First Edition

Cover and back cover design by Ron Hasler

Book interior design by Noel S. Morado

Editorial consultant Eric Brandenburg

Registered with the WGA Writer's Guild of America, Registration: 1895715

All Rights Reserved.

No part of this book may be reproduced without permission, except in cases of short quotes used in reviews and educational or critical studies.

LETTERS FROM BUD
Compiled from the memories, letters and war diary of John Brandenburg—February 4, 1946, Collected and Edited by Edith Brandenburg. Originally Published in "The Dakota Farmer," North Dakota, Spring 1947.

Photo illustrations from John "Bud" Brandenburg's private collection

A Potatohead Production

Happy Publishing

www.HappyPublishing.net

For Those Who Served

June 6, 1944

Normandy, France

" They are more to me than life, these voices, they are more than motherliness and more than fear; they are the strongest, most comforting thing there is anywhere: they are the voices of my comrades. "

– Eric Maria Remarque,
All Quiet On The Western Front

For Bud

Contents

Acknowledgements ix

Editor's Note x

Preface xi

1. **Training** 1

2. **Active Duty in Europe** 24
    - MISSION 1. ST. AVORD, FRANCE 25
    - MISSION 2. CHERBOURG PENINSULA, FRANCE 28
    - MISSION 3. LAVAL, FRANCE 30
    - MISSION 4. DREUX, FRANCE 39
    - MISSION 5. EMMERICH, GERMANY 42
    - MISSION 6. TOURS, FRANCE 43
    - MISSION 7. MELUN, FRANCE 47
    - MISSION 8. WESERMUNDE, GERMANY 49
    - MISSION 9. ST. VINOCQ, FRANCE 51
    - MISSION 10. LAON, FRANCE 53
    - MISSION 11. PERRONE, FRANCE 60
    - MISSION 12. SAARBRUCKEN, GERMANY 63
    - MISSION 13. MADGEBURG, GERMANY 65
    - MISSION 14. KIEL, GERMANY 71
    - MISSION 15. MUNICH, GERMANY 74
    - MISSION 16. SAARBRUCKEN, GERMANY 75
    - MISSION 17. CAEN, FRANCE 76

  MISSION 18. OBERPFAFFENHOFEN, GERMANY 77

3. **Breakup of the 492nd Bomb Group** 86
  MISSION 19. BREMEN, GERMANY 87
  MISSION 20. LAON, FRANCE 88
  MISSION 21. MERY SUR OISE, FRANCE 89
  MISSION 22. HAMBURG, GERMANY 94
  MISSION 23. OSTEND, BELGIUM 99
  MISSION 24. ZWISCHENHAHN, GERMANY 104
  MISSION 25. GRANIENBURG, GERMANY 112
  MISSION 26. KARLSRUHE, GERMANY 117
  MISSION 27. ULM, GERMANY 118

4. **Bud's Adventure with the Air Transport Command** 120

5. **Epilogue** 168

6. **The Koltun Crew Log Book** 174

About the Author 215

Acknowledgements

Sharing the story of our father's life during World War 2 has been a long held dream. This book could never have become a reality without the love and support of the entire Brandenburg family.

I want to thank my brothers, John (Jeb), Dan and Eric and their families for their ongoing support during the work on this project. I would also like to express my sincere thanks to my dear friends Ron Hasler and Armand Hargett, who never stopped believing in the importance of sharing Bud and the Koltun crew's story. I also want to express my gratitude to Erica Glessing of Happy Publishing for guiding the process with expertise, kindness and insight. Finally, I want to thank and acknowledge the many war veterans and survivors I met while working on this book who encouraged me to see it through, in honor of all who served.

Editor's Note

These letters, written by my father, John "Bud" Brandenburg, during his time in the 8th Allied Air Force in Europe from 1944-45, came into my possession after my mother put them in book form in 1998, following a family gathering at which a close friend publicly implored Bud to publish and share his letters (which had been sitting in an antique bureau for decades) with the world. The letters had originally been collected by Bud's mother, Edith, and were then published in a magazine called "The Dakota Farmer" in 1947. The re-edited, 1998 edition of the typewritten book was given to me, my brothers and the surviving members of Dad's air crew (the Koltun crew), who had manned the B-24 plane the men flew during their numerous missions over Europe during the war.

After receiving the letters, I began to seriously study them, reading them over and over again, each time discovering some new and vivid detail about Bud's life during the war. As I read the letters, Dad's history came vibrantly to life and healed much of the pain I had experienced after his passing in 2005. Those painful memories were transformed as, in my careful readings of his work, Dad ("Bud") became a vivid character in his own life story. Soon, every time I wanted to "visit" him, I had only to open the pages of this book to hear his voice and smile at the memory of his singular intelligence and vivid sense of humor.

I offer my boundless gratitude to his mother, Edith, and to my mother, Muriel, for their foresight in saving these letters and his diary entries. By doing so, Bud's remembrance of his war experience can now be shared with anyone curious about a young soldier's life and times during the final days of World War II.

Preface

22 in 44.

This collection of letters was written by John "Bud" Brandenburg while he served with the US Army Air Corps in Europe during the Second World War. Bud acted as a flight navigator back in the days when air navigation was calculated by math, rudimentary aircraft instrumentation and a study of the positions of the stars in the night sky. He also served on many of the missions as a bombardier. The letters and diary entries he sent home were written from April of 1944 through August of 1945 and were originally published in a magazine called "The North Dakota Farmer" in the Spring of 1947.

Bud had a close relationship with his mother, Edith, and as he began his regular correspondence from Europe with her and Bud's father, Tunis, she immediately realized the significance of Bud's war experience, as well as the quality of his writing.

A writer herself, Edith carefully read and saved Bud's letters as they came in from Europe, and she then edited them together with the entries from his war diary to create a narrative of his experiences during the final, epoch-changing years of World War II.

Bud

Bud was 22 years old in 1944. By virtue of his age and the era into which he was born, fate placed him squarely within what is now often referred to as "the greatest generation." He served in the US military during the time of the Allied Force's most active engagement in the war against Hitler, at a time when few young men could resist the call of duty. Allied air support over Europe, (most significantly during the game-changing "D-Day" attack on the beaches of Normandy, France) played a major role in turning the tide of the war, and though the experience was harrowing, Bud wouldn't have missed the opportunity to serve his country during such a significant time.

The "Hard Luck" Group

Clearly, one of the larger stories of Bud's service was his association with the "Hard Luck Group," which was the nickname for the 492nd Bomb Group. Upon entering active duty in Europe (stationed at the North Pickenham air base outside of London), Bud and the other members of his flight crew were assigned to the 492nd. This group was part of the 8th Allied Air Force and was one of many bombardment groups serving as part of the United States Army Air Forces (USAAF). These air force subgroups were similar to infantry regiments in the army.

The 492nd Bomb Group was one of the most hard-hit air force groups to serve with the Allies during World War II. The group experienced an extremely high (80%) casualty rate, with planes shot down and crew members lost with alarming frequency. The disastrous record of the 492nd Bomb Group led the government to shut down the group and disperse the "surviving" crew members into other bomb groups after just 89 days of active duty. As fate would have it, Bud and his

PREFACE

crew were off on leave in London when the bomb group became engaged in two of its deadliest missions. As Bud notes in his letters, those who later learned that he had served in the 492nd often shook their heads and wondered how it was that he and the Koltun crew had survived their membership in the ill-fated group.

Enlisting

Bud joined in the war effort after two years of study at Jamestown College in North Dakota, which he attended on a football scholarship. Bud was a state gridiron champion, but the great war effort was a life experience no able-bodied young man of the time could possibly resist. Bud's view was shared by many other men his age, as this group of young men enlisted in droves as the war effort escalated after the US joined the European Allied effort after the bombing of Pearl Harbor on December 7, 1941.

By 1944, the war had been raging on for over four years[1], with France now occupied by the Nazis and England under bombardment. Western democracy was under siege, and the call was on for young Americans to "do their duty" and give their all to vanquish the fascist threat. It was in this spirit that Bud and his friends in the Koltun crew joined the Allied war effort.

"Washing Out"

Bud attempted to become a pilot when he first enlisted, but he failed to make the cut and, as he put it, "washed out" of pilot training. Without a doubt, losing out on the chance to become a pilot in the US Army Air Corps was a devastating experience, yet the reality is that many young

---

1   WW2 is said to have begun in 1939 when the German Nazi forces (lead by Adolph Hitler) invaded Poland.

men wanted to serve as pilots in the allied effort, and the competition was fierce. Still, the experience was humiliating and Bud's scrapbook from the time contains a letter of condolence from his sister Jean, as well as a form letter from the army thanking him for a "nice try."

After taking some time off to regroup after his epic (in his mind) pilot training disaster, Bud got back in the game by re-enlisting and signing up for flight navigation school. Good navigators were sorely needed, and with his skills in math, (and innate sense of adventure) Bud naturally took to the study of navigation.

By the winter of 1944, Bud had completed navigation school and was assigned to a crew which was led by pilot Irving Koltun, of Brooklyn, New York. That spring the young men of the Koltun crew continued their course of training and prepared to embark for Europe and the beginning of active duty.

It's here that Bud's story begins.

A grid iron champion in North Dakota, Bud left football stardom behind to enlist in the Allied effort.

Form letter, but a nice gesture.

HEADQUARTERS
MERCED ARMY FLYING SCHOOL
OFFICE OF THE COMMANDANT
MERCED, CALIFORNIA

T3/JWP/sh

24 July 1943

Dr. T. O. Brandenburg
820 Avenue D
Bismarck, North Dakota

Dear Dr. Brandenburg:

You may already have heard from your son that he has been eliminated from further pilot training. He is naturally discouraged, and probably feels just now that he is a failure. He should not be discouraged and he is by no means a failure. In his disappointment, he is inclined to overlook certain facts. We feel that these are facts which both you and he should recognize, and that is why I am writing to you today.

More than a year ago, the Air Forces was faced with the urgent problem of training tens of thousands of combat pilots as quickly as possible. The finest young men in the country - your son among them - were asked to enlist for pilot training. They responded magnificently. It was inevitable that not all of these aviation cadets would complete the pilot training course. It is not possible to predict with absolute accuracy whether any individual is a potential combat pilot, no matter how intelligent, healthy or industrious he may be. Some men have an indefinable thing called "inherent flying ability" and some do not. The particular "abilities" required of a combat pilot might easily make him unsuited for some other, equally valuable, Army career. The "lacks" which your son now probably feels are responsible for his elimination from pilot training may easily prove to be the particular "abilities" which will make him a success in another field.

Your son was originally selected for pilot training because he possessed many exceptional qualifications. Those charged with his training found, however, that his progress was not sufficiently satisfactory to meet the exacting standards required for combat pilots. His case is not exceptional by any means. It is the custom to reclassify a considerable number of such students for reassignment to service where their particular qualifications will be of value to their country. In this process of reclassification and reassignment, your son may go through a period of uncertainty particularly trying to him. Your sympathy and understanding will be of especial aid in assisting him to readjust himself to work more suited to him and will greatly assist him in reestablishing his enthusiasm and self-sufficiency.

Very sincerely,

Joseph W. Pirosch
JOSEPH W. PIROSCH
1st Lt., Air Corps
School Secretary

Official letter from the army thanking Bud for a "nice try," after he "washed out' of pilot training.

A condolence letter from Bud's sister Jean, regarding his pilot training "washout."

Chapter 1

Training

The Start

*"We Circled the Tarnished Green Figure
a Few Times at About 1000 Feet"*

In April of 1944 we finished crew training at Westover field, Massachusetts and went to Mitchell field, Long Island, where we obtained a new B-24[2] and any missing equipment.

During the test flight after I had finished checking the compass by "swinging it on the gun"[3] (finding its error by means of a sun-compass) the pilot took us over Brooklyn and buzzed his home at about 500 feet. He flew down one street and up another until he found his house with his mother on the front step, waving a sheet, as we whooshed by.

One bright morning our processing was completed and we took off, singly, as parts of a large flight heading north destined

---

2 The B-24 heavy bomber was known as "The Liberator." This bomber model was designed to take over from the Boeing B-17 "Flying Fortress" bombers. The B-24 did not, ultimately, overtake the B-17, but was still a major factor in the success of the Allied bombing force during the war. Production of the B-24 was stepped up during WW 2 and this plane model was produced far more than any other during the effort. The "B" in B-24 stands for bomber. Source: www.militaryfactory.com.

3 By "swinging it on the gun," Bud was finding the difference between the measure shown by the compass and the true direction as shown on the navigational directional chart. The difference in measure is called the compass error. Source: www.splashmartime.com

for the 8th AAF[4] in England. Our Flight was the first to attempt the northern crossing that year.

Just after taking off, the pilot asked for the compass heading to Bangor, Maine, our first stop, but I gave him one that took us over the Statue of Liberty in New York Harbor.

We circled the tarnished green figure a few times at about 1000 feet. The crew wasn't very talkative and Bryan, the nose gunner, made the only comment I remembered when he warned us to "take a good look."

Two days later we flew away into the dusk from snow-covered Goose Bay, Labrador, headed across the North Atlantic[5] for Iceland.

✈

At the end of April 1944, Bud's letters home resume, as he writes regarding the beginning of the crew's journey to Europe, with stops in Iceland and Northern Ireland along the way. The boys will leave the US on April 20, and finally arrive to begin active service in England in May. In late April, Bud's letters home continue:

---

4 The 8th AAF was the 8th Allied Air Force, the bombing group established in February of 1944 to centralize command of the US Army Air Forces in Europe, under the leadership of Major General Jimmy Doolittle.
5 The northern crossing Bud refers to is the North Atlantic Air Ferry Route, which was a series of air routes over the North Atlantic Ocean. These were the routes followed to ferry US aircraft from army bases in New England over to combat areas in Europe. Airfields in Newfoundland, Labrador, Greenland and Iceland (which Bud refers to) were used as intermediate landing areas for planes on the way to England. Bud and his crew took this route directly from Newfoundland during his travels with the Air Transport Command later in his war service.

TRAINING

*Bud and a best pal prepare for active duty,
fully trained with swagger to spare.*

April 27, 1944

"The Stars Shone with a brilliance
I've Never Seen Before"

Dear Folks,

This was just another flight in most ways except for a special loneliness about it and some moments of rare beauty.

For a short time while we were between Labrador and Greenland the stars shone with a brilliance I've never seen before. I stood up with my sextant[6] and shot three of them but didn't get the fourth one for just as I was getting set the great, colored, shimmering curtain of the northern lights covered it up.

When I gazed out of the plastic dome above, it seemed as if we were hanging in space, motionless, with only blackness below, the stars sparkling on all sides while this curtain of light waved above us. It had such definite shape and form I felt like asking the pilot to take us up for a closer look. It was as if we were in an orchestra pit and this radiant curtain billowing in and out around the bottom edge of which was a fringe of all the colors in the spectrum.

During most of the trip the stars were hidden and by the time the sky cleared the sun was up, so I came in by guess and by God—and a good radio beam.

All night we flew with the white nothingness about us. Nothing visible anywhere ahead, behind, below or above. Oc-

---

6 The sextant was a navigational device used in WWII to "measure the altitude of a celestial body above a horizontal line of reference." These devices were used during the pre-computer era of WWII to help the pilot and navigator read a plane's altitude by creating a false horizon, (for those times when the actual horizon was not visible) by means of a bubble that would float in liquid inside the device.

casionally I'd flash the signal lamp[7] into the air and see the light beam like a pillar in the flying snow.

Hour after hour went by watching the compass and instruments, all alone up in front; watching my plotted positions inch themselves across the vast space on my chart called the Atlantic—hoping our radio was good, because it was all we had to go by.

You've never seen a dawn until you see that blessed sun rise over the lip of the great flat sea and see between the cloud breaks the placid water below, not nearly so terrifying now that you can see it. How different it is when you're above the overcast or in darkness and can't see it. But you know it's there waiting if anything goes wrong—thousands of empty miles of it.

I said I didn't worry—I meant about the navigation. The thing we all thought of a little is "what if those engines decide to quit—what a lot of water is down there."

At dawn I stuck my head up in the dome and looked back at the pilots who were stretching and smiling—back at this big weapon rolling along that is already getting in our blood a little—back at those four big engines on that quivering wing. They hadn't misfired all the way.

We haven't named her yet, but I wrote in pencil "I'll Get By"[8] on the nose as a temporary placation to the gods. (It is supposed to be bad luck not to have the ship named.) The co-pilot and I

---

7   A signal lamp is a lamp used for sending visual signals, usually in a form of Morse code. The lamp is also called the "Aldis" lamp, after its inventor, C.W. Aldis.
8   The song (the full title is "I'll Get By As Long As I Have You" was composed by Fred E. Alhert with lyrics by Roy Turk, in 1928. The song was recorded by many major performers, including Billie Holiday and also by Irene Dunne, in the movie "A Guy Named Joe." It enjoyed even greater success when the 1940 recording by the Harry James Orchestra (with a vocal by Dick Haymes) was released in 1944, and so it was a highly popular song at the time Bud thought to use it for the plane's name. All the planes in the AAF were given names by their crew, often inspired by popular songs or movies of the time, or by crazy stories (often off-color) that had special meaning for the men flying the plane.

had been singing the song a lot so I thought the name would do till we thought of something permanent.

Now we are in a combat theater and when they told us at briefing of "the enemy" or "Jerry"[9] and his tricks to befuddle us, coming in to England it gave me a peculiar feeling I didn't have in the states (at lectures by combat men.)

The enemy is something real now—men trying to destroy me—to jam my radio and fly me into mountains with fake bearings. Funny feeling to know that men are trying deliberately with aim and purpose, to destroy me. I've always been a little awed by Nazi efficiency and methods, but no more, not after I've seen what we have done—what a vast crushing machine we've built.

ICELAND

29 April, 44

"I Lay Rolling Around Thinking of the Three Months Just Past and The Things Crammed Into Them."

Now somewhere in Iceland and rather surprised at the bleak desolation we found. Rolling rock strewn plains stretching their treeless deadness to distant mountains that rise sharply from the fiords.

Getting to sleep here is a problem because for the first time since cadet classification[10] everyone is awake on his sack and

---

9 "Jerry" was a WW2 slang term for a German citizen or soldier.
10 Cadet classification refers to the three month training the men went through to become mission ready.

racks his mind for a joke to tell. Voices in the dark telling the old shaggy dog stories with belly laughs as infectious as smallpox. Really a merry time—tho the orderly that came in late to bank the fire was probably shocked. We finally dropped off, only to be awakened by the faraway, mounting roar of a plane coming in low, a big plane very low—it thundered over like an express train and I sprang out of bed and ran outside in bare feet and long underwear to see what went on.

The plane had turned and was coming back with its landing lights on and evidently coming to land on what looked like the rock strewn plain. However, despite our fright, the pilot knew what he was doing and came in on the runway in good order—the runway was beyond our view. So we all went back to the sack but I couldn't sleep. Maybe too much coffee at the officer's club or perhaps the pie that the cute Red Cross girl had secretly given me. I lay rolling around thinking of the three months just past and the things crammed into them and then unaccountably I remembered our fishing trip to Round Lake two years ago—and the haunted house at the end of the lake where the hosts tried to prepare a scare for us. If Bob[11] had been there that would have been our best trip.

HIKE AROUND A FISHING VILLAGE

Today, after our usual noon breakfast, someone suggested going down to the village, just visible from amp, so we got some Icelandic money to spend from the finance office and hopped a truck into town. We had to hide away in the shadows among some soldiers cause we weren't allowed off the base. We wore

---

11 Bob was Bud's older brother, Dr. Robert O. Brandenburg, who later became a heart specialist and the Head of Cardiology at the Mayo Clinic in Rochester, Minnesota.

our heavy flying jackets, Koltun the pilot, Dagood the co-pilot and little Tressler the Bombardier.

We'd been warned that the natives were unfriendly so we weren't too surprised at the glum looks of the men and the "I don't see you" attitude of the women. It was still a rude shock to feel like unwanted trespassers.

We walked down the main street of this fishing village—ogling the goods in the few stores—almost stifled at first by the rotten fish smell, but getting used to it. Along the fiord we stepped out of the bright sun into a tiny bakery and bought some cakes from two pretty, glowingly healthy young girls, who seemed a bit fussed by our presence but managed to understand enough English for the sale.

All the houses were either conventionally shaped concrete bungalows or tin-plated frame structures quite regular looking from a distance. The street was narrow and in the dock district lined with little fish reducing dumps that had piles of fish heads and scales scattered about in confusion along with rusting, broken boat equipment. The best things about the town were the hardy looking people and the cute, pink cheeked kids running around.

We noticed a cliff on the bay that invited climbing but it seemed to be on someone's property so we approached some fishermen working on a dry dock and I tried, by sign language and a lot of grunts, to ask if a climb would be all right. They finally nodded their heads despite the giggle of the co-pilot, which I try to tell him will get us in trouble some day.

So we ran and jumped among the rocks out to the end of the cape where a post was stuck in the rocks. On this I hung my hat and we all kidded around about "poor Bill, I knew him well." Then we initialed the post.

On the cliff we stood in the cool wind looking out to sea watching the fishing boats come and go and the gulls diving at the splashes of the stones in the bay.

On the way back to camp we stopped in a couple of stores and marveled again at the scrubbed faces and beautiful hair of the girls and even the old women. Some of them wore the traditional outfits which resembled funeral attire 100 years ago. Of course, the women may have actually been in mourning, I don't know.

In a hardware store we found a girl clerk who could talk to us and we kidded around buying some soap.

Outside the store who should we walk into but a carload of MPs who politely urged us back to camp and a wiser use of passes.

Thus Iceland—called the "rock"[12] by the GIs here. Anybody who is here long enough starts muttering to himself and is then called "Rock-happy." The soldiers don't seem to consider it too bad here though.

✈

Before long the crew's time in Iceland came to an end, and soon the men were back on track, heading to Europe. Finally the boys arrived in Ireland, with England, and active duty in the war finally close at hand. Ireland is a welcoming place, as Bud writes:

---

12 Iceland was jokingly referred to as "the Rock" due to its rocky landscape, formed due to the many volcanic rock formations that cover the landscape there.

SOMEWHERE IN NORTH IRELAND
(The Day After We Landed—1 May 1944)

2 May 44

"Never Have I Seen Such a Lovely Spot"

Dear folks,

I am in North Ireland after a month trip. Everyone is alive and happy.

Never have I seen such a lovely spot. It is full-blooming spring here and lots of bushes are full of yellow flowers. The whole country is a spotless park, 70-acre farms cut up by hedges and groves into 10 or 20 acre plots; little creeks tinkle along in the green grass under ancient stone bridges and everywhere is the bright green of spring.

Yesterday I came upon Ted, the wolfish co-pilot, talking to a young Irish girl with red hair and freckles and a perfect brogue. Joined by 3 more pilots and our bombardier we walked this lass along the narrow country road, chattering away, singing, picking flowers, watching the cattle grazing by the brooks and every once in a while reminding each other that we were actually in North Ireland.

This friendly girl led us to a farm where the owner refused money for some buttermilk and gladly passed the time of day. The house closely adjoined the cattle barn—both of stone and connected by a covered walk. Everything looked several hundred years old. The man and his wife could have descended in any century, I'm sure, and been at home.

TRAINING

The sun was setting as we walked back down lanes remarkable for their lack of advertising billboards or waste-paper strewn about, though at the time I wasn't conscious of what was missing.

Everyone turned back but Ted and I, who, having prior rights saw the girl to her doorstep (a side-road ½ mile from her house.) We strode back in the deepening twilight, sighing as we swept this new horizon, noting the trees outlined against the western glow, slanted by many years of western wind until they grew now as if in a high gale tho only a gentle breeze was stirring.

It's hard not to grow cornily expansive about this spot, but that's the way It gets you.

(After two days in N. Ireland we shipped across the Irish Sea and wound up in the English Midlands. Here we waited five days for assignment to a training base (I wrote this after our train ride to the Midlands).

Finally the boys arrived in England on May 4. From here they headed to England, Scotland and Ireland as their training continued in the run up to active duty over Europe. DDay is just one month away, as Bud continues his writing and correspondence home.

4 May 1944

"Recently I Saw My First Enemy Plane"

Dear folks,

We are somewhere in not-so-merry-England among people for whom I have already the greatest respect. They are poor beyond any idea one has of their condition and they are without so many essentials. The paper shortage is very noticeable. On the train we drank coffee out of tin cans instead of paper cups from peddlers on the station platform.

Recently I saw my first enemy plane, a fighter (FW 190)[13] that came skimming along just over the trees. Gave me quite a start till I saw it had English markings.

Stone SAAFRO[14]

IN THE MIDLANDS, ENGLAND
(FROM MY ARMY DIARY)

From Midlands, England, Bud continues his narrative, now writing in his diary.

Four days we have idled here in crowded discontent, sleeping, reading and writing away the time.

---

13 FW 190. The USAAF (United States Allied Air Force) used a system of tail markings, with geometric symbols and alpha numerics to identify different types of USAAF bombers. The FW 190 was the Focke-Wulf 190 Wurger, a German single-seat and single engine fighter plane that was widely used during World War II.

14 The tail marking on the plane indicates that it came from the village of Stone, close to where Bud was staying.

F-47s[15] buzz us thoroughly each day and as they come very much lower than in the U.S., it was quite a thrill when they whooshed over the first time.

That train ride from a Scottish port to here was memorable.

I recall the long, perfect stone fences climbing the rolling green hills and diving into the vales.

After hours of travel I figured we should be in London, as I called the vast expanse of cluttered, many chimneyed houses. (I found out later it was Leeds.)

We rode all night and the officers on our crew shared one train compartment and sprawled grotesquely over each other trying to sleep. I soon gave it up however and stood at the open window watching the moonlit country slip by—and this great city of dark shapes against the lighter sky. I recall the little stir that shook me when I saw the gaunt steel framework of a bomb-ruined tower and the gaps in a row of houses where the blitz[16] had struck.

Last night I set out in G.I. shoes and high spirits to walk to the local village of Stone. I walked rapidly down the right of the road thinking hard about nothing till I looked up and heard the call of birds and saw the plum trees blooming and cattle grazing on the bright green field. Then I felt rather foolish for not being

---

15 The F-47 (the Republic P-47 Thunderbolt) was a comparatively lightweight fighter plane known for its incredible diving speed, along with a huge payload capacity. Nicknamed "the Mighty Jug," the planes were regarded as "flying tanks" that could take on "staggering" punishment from the enemy, while still moving swiftly. Source: www.militaryhistorynow.com

16 The "Blitz" refers to the bombing campaign waged upon London (and other areas in England) by the German forces from September 1940 up through May 1941. This bombing campaign targeted civilian areas as well as industrial sites. The Blitz began after Prime Minister Winston Churchill ordered a bombing campaign on Berlin after a German bomb hit a civilian area in the middle of London, after missing a military target outside the city. Churchill (who believed the bombing was targeted and intentional) ordered the British bombing fleet to retaliate immediately, which set off the wave of bombings against England by the German forces. Source: www.historyplace.com

more attentive to the view. Just about the time my enthusiasm for the spring was being supplanted by a desire to get to town and a straining to see it around the bend, a taxi picked me up and I went on to the greater town of Handley.

After a few days wait at Stone we were shipped back to Hire to take a 10 day combat course. We were taught to use the new electronic device the British had developed called a "Gee" box[17]. It will give an absolutely accurate position within 30 seconds and should be a great aid in this soupy English weather. Other parts of the course included intelligence refreshers on behavior if shot down, ditching and RAF[18] navigational aids.

The following letter was written by Bud as the crew took shape and prepared for immersion in flight school. The visit to Ireland obviously gave the boys a welcome respite as they prepared for the coming air missions over Europe.

---

17 The name "Gee Box" comes from a code name that was given to The Royal Air Force's navigation system during the war. This system works by measuring the time delay between radio signals in an area. This measurement provided the navigator with a fix on a target with an accuracy within a few hundred meters. This fix could be read from a distance of up to approximately 350 miles. Source: www.vectorsite.net

18 The RAF is the Royal Air Force, the wartime air force of the United Kingdom.

TRAINING

IRELAND AGAIN

May 12, 1944

"These Bomber Crews Are Certainly a Merry, Slap-Happy Crowd"

Dear Folks,

I'm lying on my stomach on a grassy hilltop overlooking the sea and letting a cool afternoon wind rumple my hair. Alongside a nearby country road a stone fence makes its way—a very poor Irish fence compared to the Scottish ones we saw. Soldiers ride by on bikes occasionally and some stop to take pictures of a farm house 300 yards away that has a red tile roof and the usual numerous chimneys despite it being only a cottage. (This was during our stay at a coast town waiting for the combat school to make room for us.)

These bomber crews are certainly a merry, slap-happy crowd. You'd think we didn't have a worry in the world. Our gunners were unloading some stuff (off a boat) and as usual made a game of it—rushing around like mad, racing each other, throwing everything they could to each other. Along came some men of the ground forces—very glum, very business-like doing the same sort of work. After 10 minutes working by our men they caught the spirit and were having a wonderful time—much to the amazement of some Limeys who had watched the whole thing. It's cause we have so little responsibility when on the ground that we are carefree.

✈

In the dead of night our long straggly column tramped through the blacked out town (on our way to the ship that would take us back to England and combat.) Everyone talking, snatches of song breaking out, men laughing at the drizzle that started to fall as we wound in and out of the recently silent, black streets.

Someone with a flashlight noticed a sign "Brooklyn" on one of the houses so everyone yells for Koltun and he acknowledges with much praise of that city.

So we clop on with our mess-kits rattling to the edge of town where we'll sleep. Standing in the rain waiting for the camp to come alive enough to get us shelter — some smoke, some joke, some just stand. Suddenly Dagood (our co-pilot and the outfit's card) steps in front of the column and says in a commanding voice, "your attention please, at ease." Much to our surprise everyone hushes –then he asks, "Is everybody happy with the service here?" – such laughter.

On the Scottish coast while awaiting shipment to England Tres and I took a walk along the seashore near our camp. The tide was out and the sand sea floor was covered with a biologists' dream. Tres was a biology major and I had a small zoology course so we had a wonderful time trying to figure out what went on. We noticed hundreds of little piles of macaroni shaped sand and finally figured out, after a lot of guessing and digging, that these were made by clams that work like earthworms, shoving the sand through themselves and absorbing anything digestible. Also saw dozens of limpets, snails, lizards, barnacles, that reminded me of arthritis patients. The critters gradually turn to stone, you know. Many tiny crabs were everywhere and seaweed by the ton grew on the rocks. I was happy to recognize the seaweed as the very same variety which three years ago we were dissecting and studying in biology lab. The plants here were all swollen and full of spores—just about as far along in their pregnancy as the ones at school had been. We both were sorry that we hadn't learned more from the course—I could scarcely remember a single specific item about any of the things we saw—could just recall in a general way that I had seen their picture somewhere; some student.

Yesterday Tres and I stopped and leaned resting on a stone wall looking over the quaint old farmhouse just beyond. The woman of the house, about 60, came out and chatted. She was very friendly and not inquisitive that we couldn't talk to her. She told us how long the war had been and recalled the day it began. "September is a fine fair month here, but when Chamberlain[19] says the war is on at 11 in the mahrnin the sky's got black—aye, and it stormed and lightnin' flashed—it was a bad omen we said, and it was."

In some ways our army is a bunch of loud bums and I've got to hand it to the British for their self-control, but despite the often childish behavior it's a lot of fun to be with—mostly cause you can't hand these guys the old bushwah and get away with it and many act as if there could never be any serious consequences to what they do.

---

19 "Chamberlain" refers to Neville Chamberlain, Prime Minister of the UK from May 1937 until 1940. Chamberlain became notorious due to his efforts to appease and accommodate Hitler, even as Germany stepped up its invasion of Europe before the Allied forces entered the conflict. Source: www.britannica.com

One big question posed at our bull sessions is—what if the coming invasion fails? Will the now apathetic U.S. public be willing for the war to continue and the casualties to keep mounting? Most soldiers would agree it must go on to the crushing of the enemy or in 20 years we'd be on the rack again. To faraway America we doubted if the issue would be so real—what with the Chicago Tribune, etc...

Trying to figure out war aims is too tough a job from right here. Let mine suffice at fighting an obvious wrong that is bigger and more wrong than other wrongs have ever been.

Action will be little new to us—I can see myself standing there as we go through the flack[20], and saying, "Well here we are in action and it seems quite the same as we had expected." Just as over the north Atlantic I kept saying to myself, "Well here we are over the Atlantic navigating—feel different?—nope—scared?—a bit. Did you think you'd be scared?—Yes, only a lot more than I actually am."

I expect action to be tough and expect to be scared—I just mean I am prepared for what comes—I don't mean that I'll be sitting on a bombing run cool as ice.

Your letters from home fill a big need. A bit of love—a soothing word in this harsh humoured grimness—this world of proud, cynical, young men.

Right now it is eleven thirty at night—almost dark. We sit on our beds that seem to be huddled around the small grateless

---
20 "Flack" (or "Flak") are the metal fragments shot from anti-aircraft artillery.

stove in the center of our Nissen hut. The stove is not good and we miss a fire for it is cold and damp at night here. Koltun and Dagood are in bed—misshapen lumps all under the covers, even their heads. Tres has just finished cleaning up the place made dirtier than usual by the shells of some black market eggs we boiled on our little camp stove. Koltun's portable radio is on Berlin, the best music available, and we are listening to Lord Haw-Haw who certainly knows what to bang away on to split us from the British.

The crew has been together quite a time now—the officers and the first snap judgments have altered a bit. The pilot, Koltun, Polish Jew from Brooklyn is very overbearing and loud at times, but he is also very intelligent and well informed with a good sense of humor that makes living with him a lot easier. Being a first generation Pole may have something to do with it—anyhow he believes in the war mightily and is able to argue for it, a lot more than many among us can do. I like him more and more.

The co-pilot, Dagood, is tall, wavy haired, and constantly thinking of, speaking of, or chasing girls. He is easy to get along with (he gets along with Koltun yelling at him, where many a more sensitive man would have quit), but I gather more and more lately that although he'll fight because he has to he isn't very hopped up about the idea and wants to go home. Such an attitude is extremely irritating, especially when the guy tries to argue about it with as rude a set of distorted facts and corkscrew generalizations as I've ever heard. Koltun (Oiving) and I always smash him heartily into the ground in our skirmishes but he doesn't change. Prejudices take a lot of working on. Dagood is anti-semetic and the pilot is a Jew, but they are buddy-buddy most of the time, so I guess we'll get by.

Our quiet bombardier, Tressler, is a fine guy and we tag around together a lot. I'm quite fond of him. He tells long, involved, flat ending anecdotes like nothing I've ever heard. I wish I could remember one for you. Tress is eager to fight and seems as happy as any, considering he had to leave a wife of four months, one with whom he is much in love.

Thirty missions is the deal for us now, but if we can really grind down the Luftwaffe[21], it won't be too bad. Jerry is still around though, and plenty hot, despite what the newspapers say.

There is something I should mention—someday soon we will start to fly our missions. Remember that no news is good news, also that if you get one of those telegrams saying "missing," the chances are I'm a prisoner. At least half parachute in safely. German prison camps are not too ritzy but they do abide by the Geneva convention. We have a lot of their men, so don't worry too much.

We are located at Tivetshall, sixteen miles south of Norwich.

At this moment in the narrative, Bud and the Koltun crew are poised to begin active duty after their months of training, and the recent weeks of travel in England and Ireland.

As Bud's story continues, the following entry seems to have come from his diary, jumping ahead to the time after the Koltun crew's service in the 492nd had ended. Here Bud writes of the crew and their service in the past tense, noting especially that had they known they

---

21 The Luftwaffe was the German wartime air force.

TRAINING

had signed up to serve in a bombing group hit by the worst "hard luck" in the Allied Army Air Corps, they might have bailed out had they had the chance. Bud being Bud, however, he never would have abandoned his men, even if he had been blessed with such foresight.

Bud's mother, Edith, initially edited his letters after the war and combined them with his diary entries to create a narrative. It's likely that she placed this entry within the timeline of the letters (rather than as an epilogue) in order to give a better perspective on what fate had in store for the young crew.

Here Bud continues:

Finally the weeks of training and waiting were over and we were assigned to our combat group. It was the 492nd[22] of the 2nd Division and if we'd known its fate when we joined our spirits would have been considerably lower than they were.

Within a few days of our arrival they lost 14 planes at Politz north of Berlin from fighter attacks. Two weeks before they had lost 12 at Brunswick and were beginning to talk about their leadership in uncomplimentary terms.

In two months, this new group lost about 80 per cent of its original personnel mostly to fighter attacks that would sweep more than a squadron at a time from our formations in attacks that seemed to come about every two weeks. In the mean time the usual losses from flak went right on.

---

[22] Bud was assigned to the 492nd Bomb Group as part of the flight crew piloted by Irving Koltun. The bomb group was comprised of 70 original flight crews and 49 replacement crews that had at least one mission to their credit. The 492nd came in with a high reputation, as the group's pilots had experience as flight instructors and included military veterans who had manned missions up the Atlantic coast since early in the war.

As the missions wore on, the group garnered the nickname "The Hard Luck Group," due to the high numbers of casualties (80% of the group's planes were shot down in combat) experienced by the fliers. Bud mentions that the possible explanation for the high casualty level is the silver, all metal exteriors of the unit's aircraft, which made it an easy target for the German Luftwaffe.

Being a member of that group gave us a certain distinction though we all would have been happy without it. On leave we were looked on as something out of the ordinary by crew-men from other bases and the usual crack was "what are you doing alive!"

Our crew escaped these nerve-wracking air battles by simple good luck. We were always on leave when the worst flights took place. This went on during our entire stay with the group. I saw the result in empty huts and new faces on the base.

The outfit's luck finally ran out in October when it lost 29 out of 30 on one mission. This heavy blow was one of the last dealt by fighters of the German Air Force.

The narrative of Bud's observations now continues from the spring of 1944, as the crew begins training. A sense of high times and Yankee camaraderie comes through clearly in Bud's remembrances of these heady times. After the four weeks of intensive training and travel in England, Scotland and Ireland, the boys were finally ready for active duty.

Here Bud continues his description of the crew's early days in Europe.

TRAINING

May 27, 1944

"There Is A Friendly Air About This Place"

Dear Folks,

We are at our combat base, still bickering as usual but following Koltun's motto—"Anything goes boys, but don't let's be bitter."

There is a friendly air about this base—all the officers say hello to one another, stranger or not, and the GIs are surprisingly eager to salute.

The first time we saw the planes come in from a raid was quite a thrill. A few of us were standing in a railroad station waiting for a train to take us the last jump to our combat base. It was a hot, windless afternoon without a cloud in the sky and we were running around unloading baggage when we heard this droning in the sky and saw what seemed like hundreds of B-24s only a few hundred feet off the ground and in perfect little Vs[23] of three that made up squadrons of 12. The first sections swept quickly over our admiring crowd (I'd never seen more than 7 in the air at once before) and they were greeted by open-mouthed "ohs" and "ahs" from every hand. More and more followed, coming in off the North Sea, home from Germany.

---

23 The classic "V" formation (also referred to as a "skein") is the formation used by flocks of migrating birds, and was often used in flight by the Army Air Corps. The V formation is said to improve fuel efficiency of aircraft and so is regularly used in military flight missions. Source: www.wikipedia.org/wiki/V_formation

CHAPTER 2.

Active Duty in Europe

*F*inally, active duty commenced. Here Bud describes the Koltun crew's first mission, on June 2. The Allied invasion of Normandy, France, "D-Day," was just a few days away.

Bud writes:

COMBAT

June 2

"I Had A Terribly Alone and Insecure Feeling"

First mission we flew with an experienced crew just for the experience. Pilot was Haag, one of the two almost identical twins, both airplane commanders.

Flight was very short and uneventful, just to the French coast near Bologne and back, but I had a terribly alone and insecure feeling as I watched the coast of England drift back behind us as we crossed the cloud covered channel. Bombing was by radar thru the clouds.

I tried to keep out of the bombardier's way as he watched the lead ship for the moment to hit the switch. I remember the little cluster of bombs dropping slowly, gracefully, without hurry or effort away from the ship next to us—down, down, smaller and smaller, till they were just a flight of specks disappearing into the clouds.

Though there was no opposition I thought that the curving pillar of smoke left by the flare on the lead ships' bombs was the path of a Nazis rocket and I reported it to intelligence.

With one mission accomplished, active duty was now in full effect for the Koltun crew. Bud's narrative continues with a description of the next mission, two days later:

MISSION 1
ST. AVORD, FRANCE

June 4

"German Gunners On The Coast Are Very Good"

Koltun's crew together again and our first real mission—a deep plunge into South France[24]. Being quite nervous and conscientious I was so busy navigating as we crossed the chan-

---

24 Bud here mentions the South of France, which sets the stage for the oncoming DDay attack on the beaches of Normandy (offically named "Operation Overlord" by the US Military) which is regarded as the turning point in the war against Nazi Germany. When the US joined the Allied Forces, the country was coming to the direct aid of France, which had been occupied by Hitler's Nazi forces since its invasion in April 1940.

The history of France's friendship with the United States goes back a long way, from the support France gave to Washington's troops during the Revolutionary War to France's gift to the US of the Statue of Liberty. Given the long friendship shared between these countries, the Allied Force's decision to invade France in order to turn the tide of the war is a deeply profound one.

nel that I forgot to put on my heavy body armor (flak suit[25]), something I always do while over enemy territory (flak from Spain to Denmark).

German gunners on the coast are very good and to my amazement I saw outside my bubble window the oily black smoke of old shell bursts rushing by. Then a "Whump" and the tin-can-rattle of pieces going through the plane. A very close burst—and in a panic I tried to get into my armor. Foolishly in my haste and fear I put the chest protector over my interphone and oxygen leads almost strangling me as I moved around. By the time I was fully organized we were out of danger and I was in a cold sweat and the crew was hopping mad cause I hadn't answered on the interphone (my wire had been disconnected in my struggles.)

As the earth unrolled beneath us and the target moved into view far ahead, we watched another group of B-24s flying at right angles to us to bomb an airfield close to our course. It was very exciting. Flying on the course they soon put them behind us but as they dropped back we watched the stacatto, red flashes of their bombs as they hit the runways and hangers far below. The bombs came down "in train" so as to cover a great area. Smoke billowed into the air and fires started—our crew jabbered back and forth—"Did you see that?"—"Gosh!"

Then we settled down into our duties watching for our own target. The flack was not as close at this target as it was at the coast and we took rather a detached view of it, even watching the red flash of the guns below and noting where the four shells

---

25 The "Flak Suit" or "Flak Jacket" was worn by men in the 8th AAF bombers to protect them from flak (flying debris and shell fragments that came through the planes during attacks from enemy aircraft). The original jackets were given to the United States Army Air Forces from the Royal Air Force (RAF) of England, as the jackets were too bulky for the men to wear comfortably within the smaller cockpit area of the bomber planes flown by the RAF. Source: www.wikipedia.org/wiki/Flak_Jacket

from each battery broke. Between pulling my steel helmet over my ears as far as possible and dropping the bombs on the leader, I even found time to plot the ground batteries on my target map.

"Operation Overlord," which kicked off with the Allied invasion of the beaches of Normandy, France, commenced on D-Day, June 6, 1944. At that moment, the war had been raging on for five years. France was under Nazi occupation and Hitler's troops were carrying out extensive bombing missions over England. The Allied leaders knew a bold move had to be made in order to turn the tide of the war and thus the carefully planned Normandy invasion was launched.

From Bud's diary comes this first person account of D-Day, from the air. The secrecy placed around the invasion has been much noted in the war's history. Here Bud notes that the men had no idea what was coming; they were only informed of the invasion late at night on June 5. The massive Allied invasion of France took place early the next morning.

MISSION 2.
CHERBOURG PENINSULA, FRANCE

June 6, D-DAY

"We Knew Something Big Was Up"
(From My Diary)

Last night, the fifth of June, we were alerted for a briefing at 11 PM. Because of two hours of daylight savings time, it was still light out when we walked the half mile from our hut to the briefing room through the cool still air.

We knew something big was up as all the local brass was standing around. There was an exciting rumor around that we might be in on a shuttle run to Russia such as had been in the papers lately.

I'll never forget the quiet in that big room when they told us that "This is the morning we've been waiting for. Today our men are invading France." We all had a hard lump in our stomachs. Not that we were afraid for ourselves—it was the same old thing for us—but the thought of all those men in the boats walking into what we thought would be a bloody beach. We were to lay a pattern of bombs right on the beach when the boats were only 600 yards off shore.

The colonel read a message from Doolittle[26] (8th AAF Commander) and Eisenhower[27] "Don't let your bombs fall short..."

---

26 James "Jimmy" Doolittle was a pioneer in aeronautics, having worked as a pilot, engineer, leader in war combat and in military strategy. He was brought out of retirement (he served in World War I and was given the Congressional Medal of Honor for his leadership of a raid on Japan in 1940) to command the 8th AAF in its missions over Europe during World War II. Source: www.history.com/world-war-II/James-H-Doolittle

27 General Dwight D. Eisenhower was a five-star General in the US Army who served as the Supreme Commander of the Allied Forces in Europe during World War II. He was critical to the planning of the successful invasion of France and Germany during

ACTIVE DUTY IN EUROPE

We drew our courses on the maps with the other navigators. I remember how nervous the lead navigators were about making the rendezvous come out right. I remember the course formed a great figure eight[28] over England and the channel coast. Then we got into our flying suits and caught a truck out to the field in the darkness. The whole crew was already at the plane and Tres, the bombardier, was busily checking the bombs. The rest stood around talking, speculating on the invasion and fidgeting. During this time a plane from another field took off and crashed. We saw the explosion but wisely didn't talk and we were spared that jangle to the nerves.

At 0322[29] we took off and climbed into the dirty overcast to assemble on top. It was a long nerve-wracking climb and we didn't break out into the bright moonlight on top till we were above 10,000 feet.

We were the only plane to find our leader and we followed him dutifully all the way even when he jinked[30] in the early dawn joining a PFF ship by which to bomb through the clouds.

Nothing could be seen of the invasion—just solid grayness below us and I dropped Koltun's "Bomb!" by hitting the salvos bar when the toggle switch didn't work.

Quite a day—caught a little flak going by the Channel Islands.

I hope the paddle-feet do all right. How nice we have it.

World War II. After the war Eisenhower was named the Supreme Commander of NATO and served as President of the United States from 1953 until 1961. Source: www.history.com

28 The "figure 8" pattern was used in military training maneuvers, as the symmetry of the pattern made for smooth handling of the plane. Source: "Wings of Gold, An Account of Military Aviation Training in World War II," from the correspondence of Robert Right Rea, edited by Wesley Phillips Newton.

29 Military time is expressed using a 24-hour clock, thus 0322 is actually 3:22 AM on the civilian twelve hour clock.

30 In the military lingo of the time, "jinking" is a quick turn by the pilot, done in the interest of evading attack or being seen by the enemy.

After landing bleary eyed and weary, safe at home again, we hurried into the interrogation room for hot coffee and eats before officers. Instead of the usual GI handing out coffee a very pretty girl was fixing it up for us. Everyone immediately perked up and the co-pilot says "ah-English:" She said no, "American from North Dakota." I was flabbergasted of course and we instantly got down to towns and I'll be damned if it wasn't Ruth Christiensen Register. I hadn't known her, but brother Bob had and I vaguely remembered her picture in the paper and we bubbled back and forth for a moment. I finally convinced her I was actually Bob Brandenburg's brother by referring to her dad as "the old judge-wearer of the silver beaver for being the eagerest beaver in the boy Scouts." We had to rush away, and I haven't seen her since, but she was sure a morale builder.[31]

There was no time to rest even after the historic D-Day invasion of France. The crew was sent out again and the boys were back in action on June 8.

MISSION 3.
LAVAL, FRANCE

June 8

"While Waiting at The Channel We Saw The Sun Come Up"

---

31 News about the war in Europe and from the men and women serving there was of huge interest to the families back home in the US. Bud's story about his chance meeting with Ruth Register from North Dakota was big news and was written up in the local newspaper as an item of major interest at the time.

ACTIVE DUTY IN EUROPE

Night take-off again, assembly impossible due to weather. VHF (very high frequency radio) out so went to coast and waited for the group. They didn't come for an hour so in the meantime we joined another outfit and bombed an unbriefed target in France. Toggle switch[32] again out so I again salvoed[33] manually 5 seconds late and as luck would have it the leader aimed short so I think we hit.

While waiting at the channel we saw the sun come up making the water red as it shown through the haze and clouds. Unusually heavy condensation trails that day forming regular clouds, very striking especially in a formation turn.

The leader we were with on this hop flew around for half an hour over France with his bomb bays open causing me to sit straining on the floor trying to watch his bay to see the first bomb out so I could drop. With my eyes glued to him and never relaxing I couldn't navigate and as a result we never did locate the target we hit (for the intelligence men, though, we looked at pictures for an hour the next day).

We landed from this mission in a thick haze and only got in after two passes at the field while dodging other planes coming in. Kusker, (pilot friend from Westover) was commended for landing his B-34 dead stick[34] when all four engines ran out of gas at once as he circled the field. With admirable presence of mind, he wracked the big bird over and landed crosswind with only minor damage, nobody hurt.

---

32 A toggle switch is used to open up or close off an electrical circuit, through the use of a level. Source www.398th.org/Research/398th_FAX.html
33 To "salvo" is defined (by Merriam-Webster) as "the release all at one time of a rack of bombs or rockets" — as from an airplane.
34 A "dead stick" landing refers to a landing that is forced when the plane loses all its power. The "stick" is a reference to the plane's wood propeller, which is a "dead stick" when the plane is without power.

LETTERS FROM BUD

✈

After the intensive training period and the first run of missions in Europe, Bud began to bond with the other men of the Koltun crew. In his letters home after D-Day, he finally finds time to detail the unique qualities of his new friends as he writes to his mom and dad.

CREW

June 9

"I Wish The Men Got On As Well As We Officers Do"

Dear Folks,

Here are the enlisted men on the crew.

Murphy—engineer—a rather sour lad from Oklahoma who seems to have a persecution complex and whose disposition has not endeared him to the other enlisted men, especially.

ACTIVE DUTY IN EUROPE

The crew lives it up while on leave.

Chandler—tail gunner[35] from Wisconsin—whose cocky, slaphappy way has gotten him into innumerable scrapes. His personality is such a contrast to Murphy's that there is friction. In the air he is very nervous, wants to abort (turn back) if there is anything wrong with the ship. His buddy is Bryan.

Bryan is a tall good-looking waist and nose-gunner from Texas. He is the best sergeant we've got, very eager to learn despite being a washed out cadet[36]. He gets along with everyone, but little is known of his life except that he is very rough and ready and shares Chandler's escapades.

Jacobson—is assistant engineer and top turret gunner. Shy, much embarrassed little family man from Wisconsin also. He and Murphy form one clique, Bryan, Chandler and Grab, another. He is our ball turret gunner[37] from Wisconsin, is older and wiser than the rest of the men and uses his head in the bickerings. Also married.

---

[35] The Tail Gunner position on a military aircraft was placed at the rear—or "tail" of the plane. The right waist gunner was stationed at and fired a gun from the window just behind the right wing. Similarly there was a left gunner stationed on the other side of the fuselage. There was also a tail gunner stationed in the tail. The ball turret gunner was stationed below the plane fuselage and the top turret was stationed on top behind the pilot. The bombardier and navigator also fired guns from the nose section. Source www.398th.org/Research/398th_FAX.html

[36] A cadet who "washed out" is one who failed to make the cut in pilot training. The attrition rate for cadets in pilot training during WW II was 40%, with many men either failing to pass during one phase of training, or being killed during the rigorous flight training. Many of the "washed out" cadets later enrolled in training as navigators and bombardiers (as did Bud). Source: www.wingsofhonor.org

[37] The position of the ball turret gunner was immortalized in the Randall Jarrell poem, "The Death of the Ball Turret Gunner," which, in five lines, captured the poet's experience of the darkness of war, as he likened the position of the man in the round "ball turret" to a child in the womb, washed out when the birth was aborted.
Jarell, who served in the Army Air Forces during WWII wrote of the ball turret position:
"A ball turret was a Plexiglas sphere set into the belly of a B-17 or B-24, and inhabited by two .50 caliber machine guns and one man, a short small man. When this gunner tracked with his machine guns a fighter attacking his bomber from below, he revolved with the turret; hunched upside-down in his little sphere, he looked like the fetus in the womb."
Source: https://en.wikipedia.org/wiki/The_Death_of_the_Ball_Turret_Gunner

Gilmore—young, intelligent, eager and courteous radio operator is so eager to help he gets in his own way. Comes from Massachusetts and has a twang to his speech. Stands by himself, helpful and co-operative but quite independent, not sharing in the adventures of the harum-scarum boys.

It doesn't sound so good for a crew to be divided among itself but they all co-operate in the air and that is what counts. I wish the men got on as well as we officers do but I'm afraid the conditions won't change much. Since we've been in combat Murphy's attitude has improved but no one is very fond of him. Jacobson strings along with him cause he is directly over him. No thought of getting rid of him as the thorn in our nest but decided not to cause he does his job, seems to be improving and you can't tell what you might get.

The other night the co-pilot and I rode bikes into town along these country lanes. I noticed a lovely stone church (village of Swafham) and stopped a moment in the yard to part the tall grass about the tombstones and read the dates on the weathered old stones. "We loved you much but Christ loved you best—1835." The church looked very old but was well made and in good shape. It reminded me of a miniature cathedral with gargoyles staring down here and there.

British pubs are a very nice part of the British workman's life. I like the atmosphere in them. Often they'll be in a house that looks like a home but for a rusty old sign such as "The Horse and Groom" or "The Lion's head."

In one room will be a bar where they serve milk and bitter stout, British beer served flat at room temperature. Often the bar is merely a plank and the barman simply turns to the barrel behind him and fills your glass.

A poor man's place, sometimes a pint glass for 6D or 10 cents, usually a shilling or 20 cents. Off the bar room are other rooms very poorly furnished with battered walls and furniture. In one you'll find a group of workmen at a table talking, probably politics, but I've never seen them noisy on any subject. In another usually crowded room will be a crowd of young people about a broken-down off key piano. ATS girls (English WACs) and British sergeants with a liberal amount of Yankee non-coms. The most surprising thing is to see seated along the walls old grandmothers chattering away to each other and sipping their ale. Very friendly and completely at home. I've never seen a civilian drunk in a pub though the soldiers of both countries get pretty loud sometimes.

Although there's no place else in town to go for company we don't spend much time in the pubs. One night we walked into one in which enlisted men and British civilians were having quiet chats and the moment we walked in all talking ceased and a very uncomfortable hush fell on the room. The English aren't used to officers and men in the same place, or so we interpreted the hostility. At other times though we haven't been noticed. Depends on how much beer has been consumed by all, perhaps. I've not found the English to be especially reserved. They hate a loud oaf as much as anyone of course—a little politeness and respect for their right is all they ask.

All these observations are from two trips to town taken mostly for the exercise. We just can't get in very often and I'm saving so much money I'll have to start sending home extra.

The war presented heady times for three spirited young soldiers on leave.

Most of the time I just pedal around in town trying to sense an adventure, finally returning as darkness closes in, quite exhausted.

Someday we may see London. I've been within three miles of it but it was straight down[38].

---

38 Here Bud jokingly refers to the Allied airman's "bird's eye view" of the war. They saw and experienced Europe in many ways during the conflict, sometimes on the ground but often, as he says, from "three miles high."

RELIGION

"Before A Mission The Chaplain Gives A Prayer"

Well, folks, I have finished Tom Paine's "Age of Reason"[39] and highly recommend it to you all. He expresses so well what a lot of people really think on the subject of Christianity.

Before a mission the chaplain gives a prayer[40] which serves more as a depressant than anything else. Whenever I get prayed over like that I get a last mile feeling[41] — especially since he's one of those sallow faced, piety-jane characters with a "dying of TB" voice. I could sure go for one of Hambllin's appeals to reason if he's still dealing them out. I'd rather be told by him to gather myself together on the bombing run and kill as few Frenchmen as possible, than have this joe tell us our necks are immune cause the flak shies off at a Christian. He always closes with "and now

---

39 Thomas Paine, one of the "Founding Fathers" of the United States, was also a distinguished political writer, activist and philosopher. His influential writings helped to provoke the American revolution, when rebels broke away and declared their independence from Britain's monarchy.
Paine's "Age of Reason" was a highly influential essay that was distributed in pamphlet form. It was a lengthy thought piece that challenged the ideas behind organized religion and even the legitimacy of the Bible. (Source: https://en.wikipedia.org/wiki/ThomasPaine

40 World War II has sometimes been referred to as "the last Christian war," and it's interesting to note the many times Bud (and the log book author) refer to prayers with the army chaplains before and after their missions. At the time it was likely taken for granted that the boys who served followed the Christian religion, which in the multi-cultural environment of the new millennium would not be automatically assumed.

During World War II, (as in all the wars dating back to the Revolutionary War) some men avoided active duty by declaring themselves Conscientious objectors if they objected to serving in a war on moral or religious grounds. During World War 2 those soldiers who qualified for active duty were sent to serve in the Civilian Public Service Program, where they were assigned non-combatant "work of national importance" in the service of the army. One group of approximately 6,000 conscientious objectors, however, (mostly Jehovah's Witnesses) was sent to prison for refusing to comply in any way with the rules of the Selective Service.
Source: https://www.swarthmore.edu/library/peace/conscientiousobjection/

41 That "last mile" feeling, as in, the last mile is always the toughest part of the journey.

may the secret desire of every heart be fulfilled." You couldn't guess what the desire is.

Gee—how'd I get like that. It's a dull gray day and the skies have been weeping on us—maybe it's contagious.

✈

After this brief respite in the English countryside, the crew was assigned to another mission over France. Bud's letters continue as the Koltun crew travels to Dreux, France. Here is the mission, in Bud's telling:

MISSION 4
DREUX, FRANCE

June 12

"The Nazis Were Right On Us"

Twenty-four 250 pounders for an airport at Dreux, France—all in the target. Beautiful day though flak at the target and at Caen on the invasion coast which they told us would be taken by the time we got back. Leader took us right over the town thinking it was now ours but the Nazis were right on us and the black puffs were fairly close. Flew without Tres who was taken to be on a lead crew.

✈

Here Bud continues his overview of his experiences thus far, and his perspective on the success, just days before, of the Normandy, France,

"D-Day" invasion. It's clear from his writing that he and his parents all considered the invasion, and the war in general, an effort supported by the whole of the American public. As ugly as the war was, Bud never wavered in his loyalty to his men and to the Allied effort.

June 13

"We're Not Allowed To Reveal Our Targets"

Dear Folks,

We've been flying enough and have bombed enough to allow us to say our training was not in vain and that as far as the Army or Government goes, we've been a good investment. Always in the air corps there is the fear of training accidents—that you will be lost in vain and for nothing—now that, at least, is past.

We're not allowed to reveal our targets or any data but if you read the papers you get the general idea of our day's work. I'm bombardier on our crew in addition to navigator. Means no change in my duties as I was dropping the bombs anyway. As you can read in Life or "Target Germany"[42] every plane doesn't bomb with a bomb-sight and bombardier, only the leader uses a bombardier, the rest of us drop by flicking a switch when they see the leader's bombs start down. It is a very effective method if in tight formation and the lead bombardier is good. Precision

---

42 Life Magazine was a highly popular newsmagazine published by Henry Luce's Time/Life Corporation. Life magazine provided Americans with detailed news and photos of the war effort during the pre-television era. The magazine was generally well researched and featured vivid photo journalistic pieces created by the top writers and photographers of the time.

"Target Germany" was an informational book published by the US Army Air Force, detailing "the official story of the VIII Bomber Command's first year over Europe.

bombing is an actuality though sometimes weather hampers effective sighting or we have difficulty finding the target.

Tres, my bombardier, is no longer on the crew as he was taken to be assistant navigator on a lead crew. Bombardiers are trained in ground observation and that's his job, identifying the target and doing pin-point pilotage. A good deal for the kid cause he felt useless on our plane with nothing to do. We hate to lose him.

We've really had an amazingly easy time of it as far as opposition goes, just like missions at Westover only the sky is dotted with planes and there is a little flak. The whole crew gets a hoot out of hitting a target. By the way, they are working and getting along much better now—the sour boy seems to have taken on a little of the combat fever. So far it has been safer here than in training because the planes are maintained so wonderfully.

The success of the beachhead[43] has gladdened us all as I suppose it has you, though the way to go yet is long and rough. You should see the magnitude of the effort being exerted. The channel is choked with ships. The men on the ground and in the low-flying planes have our respect and gratitude.

After the mission to Dreux, the crew was sent to Emmerich, Germany.

---

43 The "beachhead" Bud refers to is the point on the beach in Normandy where the Allies established their position, driving back the Nazi forces in France.

MISSION 5
EMMERICH, GERMANY

June 14

"I Got Pretty Bewildered Navigating"

Twenty-four 250 pounders for an oil refinery at Emmerich, Germany, our first target in the Reich[44], near the Dutch border on the Rhine. Partial undercast and I got pretty bewildered navigating. Almost froze when my suit burned out again. Didn't use the toggle switch, it has been so often fouled up. Instead salvoed on the leader's first bombs and think we hit though most of the group's bombs went in a field.

✈

From Germany it was back to France for the crew, and Bud here offers a detailed description of the events in Tours:

---

44 During the Nazi era, under the leadership of Adolph Hitler, Germany was referred to as "The Third Reich." "Reich" is literally translated as "realm" in German, but it more universally means a time of empire. The Nazi era was the third "Reich" or third time of German Empire. The first Reich was the period of the Holy Roman Empire (1902-1806), the Second Reich was the period from 1871 to 1918. The Weimar period, from 1918-1933 was regarded by the Nazi regime as an aberration, and the era was mostly ignored in their history of German empire. Source: www.en.m.wikipedia.org

MISSION 6
TOURS, FRANCE

June 15

"We Didn't Get Any Punctures"

Twelve 500 pounders for a bridge at Tours, France. The bridge was just a hair line across the river from our 20,000 feet (location)... (they hit) in a colorful pattern but all the bombs fell on one side or the other, just like a knife through an apple (the way the bridge looked.) It was heartbreaking but no one could be blamed, just bad luck cause the sighting was as accurate as it could be with the present equipment.

On the way down we were attacked by our first enemy fighters. It was all over in five seconds and I didn't even know it was happening, being busy at my maps and computers at the moment.

Dagood, the co-pilot, saw this Messerschmidt[45] barreling down on us in a head-on attack but was so paralyzed with fear he said he couldn't say a word till the fighter had whizzed by about 50 feet above us. The nose-gunner, Bryan, had seen the plane coming in at us but by the time he was swinging the turret on it and had tried to shoot without having his gun switches on, it was too late. He was so mad at having missed a shot because of a stupid error like that that he began to call P-51s, 109s and shot at one. Gunners on the other ships gave him some unmistakable advice when he landed. The nose guns going off always frighten me very much cause they are so close and surprise me when I'm working.

---

[45] "Messerschmidt" refers to planes built by the German aircraft manufacturer Messerschmidt AG.

Tressler was in the nose of the land ship just ahead of us and was wide awake. He got in a long burst at the bandit but doesn't know if he got any hits. The German put a cannon shell in his wing-tip, but it was luckily a dud.

We didn't get any punctures.

✈

Bud continued writing that day, obviously eager to share all the news as well as his observations on the war effort with his folks.

June 15

"The Nerve Wracking Pace of Fly-Sleep-Fly-Sleep Continues"

Dear Folks,

The Luftwaffe in France is in a bad way, I should not care to be among them. Our superiority in numbers is overwhelming and we have the edge in quality of machines though it is not a wide edge.

Every day we fly over their ruined airfields—so bomb pocked and desolate they look like pictures of the moon. Whoever planned our present air force deserves more credit than he can ever receive.

The nerve-wracking pace of fly-sleep-fly-sleep continues with an occasional God given rest because of the weather. After five days in a row everyone is chewing everyone else's head off at the slightest provocation, but despite the bitching at these continual 1 a.m. awakenings, we realize how much the paddle-feet on the beaches depend on us.

Luftwaffe Gone, Yank Flier Says

Reason to believe the German Luftwaffe is for the most part depleted was pointed out today by Lt. John Brandenburg, of Bismarck, N. D., Flying Fortress navigator, who didn't see a Nazi plane in the sky in his 30 missions over Europe.

Brandenburg

Visiting friends here, the airman said the most impressive thing to him about war was the precision and magnitude with which the Eighth air force in England operates.

So heavy are the bombing raids inflicted on Germany that the entire midlands of the country appears to be going up in smoke, Brandenburg said.

Winner of the distinguished flying cross and the air medal with three oak leaf clusters, he described the excitement of one mission when the bombs became tangled with the control cables, throwing the ship into a dive and out of formation. The ship almost had to burn out its engines to get back to the rest of the group, he said.

Newspaper article reporting a visiting soldier's views on the current situation in Europe

The British press is very enthusiastic at the way we've knocked out the enemy's airfields and ruined his bridges and marshaling yards until his beachhead forces are receiving only a trickle of the reinforcements they need to stop us.

2120 HOURS

Just got in from a ride on my brand new bike; Tres and I each bought one this p.m. eight pounds and ten shillings or $34.00, (Girls' bikes but all we could get.)

An hour ago I got on mine and headed for the open road, not caring where I went and I took whichever fork in the road I chanced closest to. Laboring up and shooting down these rolling green hills with my leather jacket flying and my hat on the back of my head, I was good MP[46] bait.

Cattle were lying in the fields looking as happy as cattle ever look—unmindful of the trickle of streams and the beauty of their home.

There is a continual haze over England that makes all distant church steeples seem cathedral-like and gives a mysterious come-hither look to the country just up ahead so that you race to get to it and reveal its secrets.

I rode for miles through several tiny villages and by many ancient roadside taverns. The houses in the villages seemed to have grown from their sites. Covered with vines and with a sagging straw roof they seemed almost as alive as any tree.

The villagers were digging out in their gardens; many have lovely flowers in their front yard. You see few lawns—that is

---

46 MP refers to the Military Police Corps, which is the law enforcement branch of the United States Army.

only for the better class. All the people gave me a cheery nod as I went by.

In one settlement I drove up a winding path to the old stone church which was the same sturdy gothic that they all are—great trees spread their branches over the churchyard making a subdued and reverent light among the gravestones.

I like these little pilgrimages by myself. If I go with the lads, they want to hurry right into our village.

Poppies are in bloom on all the roadsides and dismounting to pick some I noticed a great searchlight over the hedge—set out in the green field with all its elaborate controlling and power gear scattered about.

I still say it is a nice way to fight a war.

Two-day pass to London coming and boy! are we ready for it.

✈

After the two-day pass to London, the crew was back on duty, returning to France for another mission over Melun. Here's Bud's colorful description of the mission to Melun, France:

MISSION 7
MELUN, FRANCE

June 17

"I Jumped To My Little Bubble Window To Watch The Bursts"

Twelve 500 pounders dumped on an airfield 15 miles south-west of Paris. Solid undercast most of the time and I had to struggle along with dead reckoning and the forecast winds. Did all right, however.

In my compartment on the plane on each side is a concave plexiglass window which enables us to look straight down. These bubble windows give the plane a kind of bug-eyes look but are very useful to the navigator.

On this mission we ran into some accurate flak and we heard it slamming into the thin skin of old "I'll Get By," (the plane we usually have.) We came a little close to Chartres on the way back and the top gunner called out "flak at nine o'clock"[47] (to our left) as we rode along somewhat relaxed above the clouds.

I jumped to my little bubble window to watch the bursts, up to now a fascinating sight. The quadruple bursts were fairly close. I turned back to my table when "wham!" a jagged piece of metal about an inch long shot through the window where my head had been, showering pieces of plexiglass about. I sat down and didn't feel like looking anymore.

There was no letup for the boys in June of 1944; from France it was on to a terrifying mission over Germany. Here's Bud's description of the nail-biting mission by Wilhelmshaven, Germany, in which three of the squadron's three planes were shot down, and the Koltun crew's plane, the "I'll Get By" came back with thirty-five flak holes.

---

47 The "o'clock" designation refers to the positioning of a target as it relates to the positions of the numbers on a clock. A "9" would be on the left side, as on the clock face.

MISSION 8
WESERMUNDE, GERMANY

June 18

"Everything Was In Confusion"

Most terrifying ride yet. Mission was supposed to hit an airfield at the base of the Denmark peninsula but because of severe contrails and scattered clouds we couldn't find the target without a radar ship. The squadrons in the group became separated and we found our nine ships all alone milling around near the naval bases of Lubeck and Rostock. The navigation was fairly simple because of the coastline and numerous lakes as long as we stayed away from the target area.

Everything was in confusion, no one knew what the leader would decide to do, himself least of all apparently, for we went by Lubeck once just out of flak range and then again.

Finally, we held one heading and I answered the pilot's question as to a probable target by saying we were heading west, apparently giving up the mission or else going to bomb the North Sea naval bases. This latter idea made us all a little jumpier since these great sub bases are notoriously well defended.

We continued to head west and were apparently bound for Bremerhaven. It seemed like madness for we had only a load of fragmentation bombs. But on we came and I gave the crew an estimated time for arrival. Now the base and the river were in sight and the leader's bomb bay doors rolled up.

The sky above the city was speckled with old flak bursts.

Things began to happen too fast to remember them—my eyes were glued to the leader for I had no idea when he would drop or on what. I have a vision of the Wesser River and the docks below the leader's belly when he went into a violent steep bank to the left at the same time salvoing his lead. Me too. Our motors whined in dissonance as Koltun poured on the coal trying to keep up with the leader now going south down the river. The trails of German rockets and smoke markers from our planes crisscrossed the air above the river. The leader had turned so violently to avoid leading us into the path of another squadron that had come in to bomb.

Fairly well shaken up and mad at the whole affair we closed our bomb doors and rode along in formation again. We'd walked into a hornet's nest of Allied planes—evidently this was the day for Germany's naval bases to get it.

After about 60 miles going south, we nine lonesome and bewildered crews headed back north again on a new course. After a few minutes I called the pilot, "Hang onto your hats, man, cause if the dope leading us keeps on this course we'll go right over Wilhelmshaven." On we droned above broken clouds with my nervousness increasing by the minute as we drew nearer to the great base.

Now we could see it on its peninsula between the sea and the river. Why did the leader take us over it? I haven't figured it out yet though one theory was that it was too crowded with other planes up there to make a formation turn.

Never have we seemed to move so ponderously and slowly as passing over that base. I looked straight down on the great dry docks with the ships in them being repaired, while six-inch shells broke around us with a red flash and a little black smoke. I usually tried to say something cheering over the interphone while in the flak but words wouldn't come and I just stood there trying not to watch the bursts but hearing the close ones "whump" and pieces clatter through the ship. I was ready for bed when there was finally only water below us but we still had to get home and alone at that for our hydraulic lines had been holed and to fix them the pilot dove the ship to a lower altitude over the sea so he could work without being encumbered by an oxygen mask.

We got home with no one hurt—three of our nine planes didn't. One crashed in England, two ditched unsuccessfully in the North Sea.

Had 35 holes in ship, one big chunk in my bullet box.

Even after such a gut-wrenching adventure, there was no rest or break in the action for the boys of the Koltun crew. By next morning, the crew was back on a mission in France.

MISSION 9
ST. VINOCQ, FRANCE

June 19

"The Interphones Suddenly Came Alive"

Assembly usually takes about 40 minutes. The planes get information with the leader at a radio station. During this time I have little to do and today I was looking at my bubble window. Looking back at me was a great eye perfect in detail even to the pores and blemishes on the eye-lid. It was just a greatly magnified reflection of my own eye of course, formed by the severe concavity of the window but I spend several moments of each day now looking and winking at myself with my monstrous glim while we assemble.

Mission was a milk run and mighty welcome. Bombed rocket emplacement thru a solid undercast over north France and Belgium. Bombs were hundred pounders and ten of them hung up when I salvoed. We returned with them.

A number of other planes had the same trouble and crossing Belguim above the vast whiteness we watched the plane next to us dribble out one bomb and then another as the crew struggled to clear the bomb bay. Ours was secure so we left it be.

Approaching our base at about 2000 feet, sweeping along over the fields and villages of England the interphones suddenly became alive. "Hey, men, bombs are falling out of the lead ship." The bombs were safety-ed but it still was a rather unhappy thing to scatter the missiles about, we all thought.

The pilot did more than just think about it. He yelled in the mess hall at the lead pilot. "What's the idea of bombing England?" The pilot addressed almost took a poke at him but managed to let it go. Koltun is on their list, though, for his outspoken ways and we'll never be a lead crew[48].

---

48 Bud observed that the Koltun crew would never be named a squadron leader. A squadron formation had 36 planes, and all the planes would drop their bombs at the same time, according to orders set down by the headquarters of the 8AAF. The bombardier on the lead plane, however, was the only one that actually had a bomb sight. The other bombardiers would follow the lead's timing and would release their bombs only after the lead released theirs. This design was put in place to create a maximum concentration of bombs in one target area. Source: www.398th.org/Research/398th.FAQ.html.

LETTER HOME FOLLOWING
THE CREW'S FIRST PASS TO LONDON

MISSION 10
LAON, FRANCE

June 23, 1944

"Wise Or Experienced People Stay Off The Blacked Out Streets"

This first two-day pass had been in the air for some time as we've flown a very great number of missions for the time we've been here, but we were happily surprised anyway to see our names on the bulletin board.

We stepped off the train in London rather lost and without any definite plan of action and listened to the sad wail of the sirens as the approach of yet another rocket bomb was heralded.

The day was well spent by the time we were settled in a Red Cross officer's club and had been oriented with the aid of several maps. Our place was only about five blocks from Trafalgar Square and about three from the corner of Picadilly and Regent Street. Just across the street from us was a burned and blasted old church, only one of many we saw.

A friend enabled me to meet a rather nice English girl and with Koltun and Dagood and their women we dined and danced at an English club. My date turned out to be of the upper crust and lived in a rather luxurious suite with her family.

I bade the clan goodnight and gave them every assurance that I could find my way back unaided though we had walked far from the small area I was then acquainted with.

I said goodbye, the door closed on the cheery light and I was alone in the blackness of the London night. After five minutes of stumbling about, I managed to pick up the checkered curbings and by watching the chimneys against the skyline I could tell the street's position though sometimes a lamp post would loom suddenly and give me a scare.

Wise or experienced people stay off the blacked-out streets and I had them to myself. After a bit my eyes could see more in the darkness and I started to stride out with the usual jauntiness, saying "John, it's midnight and you're in London," while my heels clicked rhythmically down the street.

Soon I was getting on further down in the congested area where the buildings are higher and thus the streets are darker. Imperceptibly I became aware of a droning buzz from the sky which my subconscious mind dismissed as just a plane. But then as the sound rose in volume and I noted its peculiar beat I stopped walking and whispered "it's a rocket"[49] to myself as my skin began to prickle.

I stood a moment and then kept walking slowly not knowing exactly what to do while that devilish thing kept buzzing, sometimes fading away and then returning. I kept sweeping the narrow aisle of sky above the street, but could see nothing. Suddenly I heard people calling to one another and running on the sidewalks, while the droning above us grew louder and louder. Then it stopped. I grabbed a railing and waited in the sudden stillness—five seconds and then the street flared into view as from lightning-another four breathless seconds and a long roll-

---

49 The "rocket" Bud refers to is a buzz bomb. These early "drone" missiles were used by the Germans to attack Londoners during the blitz. Years after the war undetonated buzz missiles were still turning up in neighborhood areas in London. In her autobiography, "Home," singer Julie Andrews describes the experience of having the people in her neighborhood constantly on alert for incoming bombs, even as "everyday" life continued during the war.

ing "whom" shook the street. Not very loud but I could sense the power of that concussion. I thought of the people in some house a mile away, buried under their own home for few go to the shelters. Their motto is "If it's going to get you, it'll get you."

Further on I met a RAF sergeant and a civilian friend and with the loquacity that spectacles or disasters always bring out, we talked freely of the missions and the rockets, occasionally stepping into doorways and huddling together as we heard the rocket motors stop.

Altogether I heard four go off before I got home with the kind aid of the Englishman.

From my room I walked out on the balcony high above the old houses of London and watched the searchlights probe the undercast fruitlessly for the 2200-pound nuisances and finally give it up.

The alert had been all night and was still on when we hit the hay.

The people take these things with admirable calmness though many told me they'd rather have a regular bomber with a crew. They said there's something eerie about that manless unthinking machine blundering around over the heart of a great city and finally falling to its destruction in the soft brick flesh of this old place.

One old fellow said he never went to the public shelters during a buzz bomb raid because, "To get me the blinking thing has got to come down Regent Street, across Piccadilly, turn sharp right at Jermyn Street and go three houses beyond the pub on the corner; how can this brainless bomb find the place when I can't myself sometimes?"

The next morning Tres and I hired an old cabbie to give us a quick tourist's view of the sights and that's just what we got.

London is not a beautiful city at all. It has no spacious avenues and its marble temples seem cluttered. It is built almost entirely of brick and everywhere you go are the gashed walls and staring shells of blitzed buildings.

The cabbie explained things to us always using "he" when speaking of Hitler or the Luftwaffe. He surprised us by showing around St. Paul's and on the Thames how "he" hit the warehouses and docks that feed London. We were rather professionally interested to see that the German's bombing hadn't been as bad as we'd thot.

Of course, terrific casualties were caused in the slums of the east and because these slums adjoin the docks and they were after the docks with the usual shorts and longs that make life near a military objective rather rugged any time.

We spent about an hour in St. Paul's. Our national capital and just about every state capital are copies of this cathedral. The idea that it looked like a capital ruined the idea that it was a cathedral.

Naturally many of the best furnishings are removed and parts of the place are bricked up for protection. One wing was roped off, but we looked across the barrier at the great hole in the roof and floor made by a mislaid bomb. Over the main altar is the huge dome covered with paintings from the life of St. Paul. In the crypt, below level, are the bones of many of England's great, including the Duke of Wellington and Lord Nelson. In this same crypt we saw the funeral car of Wellington, a monstrous vehicle made of captured cannon that reminded me of nothing so much as the juggernaut that the Hindus throw themselves beneath.

For the most part this great church is a soldier's memorial. Upstairs and down we saw classic full flowing marble groups commemorating the death in battle of someone who "raised the power and wealth of the empire to a degree never before obtained by the grace of God," and so forth. Everywhere were greater than life-size statues of dying Britons begin carried away by soft-bosomed, though marble Greek goddesses. Cathedrals and empire soldiers just don't mix.

We rode on in our cab—"Here's Charles Dickens' Old Curiosity Shoppe, founded 1557, and here's the Bank of England (the old lady of Threadneedle Street) and there's the Tower of London," which surprised me by being quite a rambling old place. "And here's a memorial to merchant sailors of the last war—and here's one for guardsmen of two wars ago," etc. Here is the Thames—this is the funny old Tower bridge—this here is London Bridge and that is the new Waterloo Bridge."

Along the Thames we came in view of the lacy spires of Big Ben and houses of Parliament and across the street we stopped at Westminster Abbey where the really great of England lie.

The Abbey is a beautiful old Gothic cathedral crowded now with the must of greatness from many ages. You could gaze here for hours, there are statues and inscriptions in abundance.

In the damp coldness beneath the pointed arches we walked slowly reading on the walls and on the floor beneath our feet. Dickens, Kipling and Hardy[50] lie here and there was a unique

---

50 Dickens, Kipling and Hardy were titans of English literature. Thomas Hardy was a poet and novelist ("Far From the Madding Crowd," "Tess of the d'Urbervilles"), Kipling ("The Jungle Book") a master story teller (raised in India and England) who won the Nobel Prize for Literature in 1907. Charles Dickens, author of "David Copperfield," "Oliver Twist" and many other masterful novels, was also a trenchant social critic, whose work provided a scathing commentary on the poverty and terrible working conditions that existed in England at the time. He is regarded as the greatest novelist of the Victorian era, and his books are still widely read today.

little statuette of Shakespeare holding a scroll on which was written, "Nations will fall, the great will pass as clouds" or something like that. His bones are still at Stratford.

Rather by itself, as is proper, is a niche to Isaac Newton[51]. I stood on the stone slab in the floor that marks his place. Beneath my feet lay all that is left of that wonderful brain. I slapped my bombardier Tres on the back, "Think," I said, "I'm standing on the handful that remains of Isaac Newton" –Tres graciously looked thoughtful.

Later we saw Buckingham palace with its windows blasted in—and sometimes we'd see crowds looking at the newest bomb ruins.

In the p.m. I saw a matinee performance of "There Shall Be No Night" with Alfred Lunt and Lynn Fontaine[52] who were superb. Scene was laid in Greece instead of Finland, due to the changed Russian situation. Much talk and no new ideas. During the performance an electric sign flashed on telling the crowd an alert was on and that there were shelter in the basement. No one left but a combination of circumstances made things pretty tense for a while.

You see, during the play there is supposed to be a bombardment and they had a sound device to imitate a bomber. Unfortunately it sounded just like the buzz bomb instead of a plane and had all the audience including me sinking down

---

Sources: https://www.poetryfoundation.org/poems-and-poets/poets/detail/rudyard-kipling, https://www.poetryfoundation.org/poems-and-poets/poets/detail/thomas-hardy, http://www.bbc.co.uk/history/historic_figures/dickens_charles.shtml

51 Isaac Newton was of course the great mathematician, astronomer, philosopher, physicist and overall great thinker who influenced the scientific revolution and the development of modern science.

52 Alfred Lunt and Lynne Fontanne were two of the most acclaimed stage actors of their time. They were married for 55 years, since 1922, and appeared in over 24 major stage productions together, including Noel Coward's "Design For Living" (which was actually written for them) Source: https://www.britannica.com/biography/Lunt-and-Fontanne

ACTIVE DUTY IN EUROPE

into our seats a little and wondering whether the real thing was on its way or not. Leaving the theatre, I felt like pinning on a campaign ribbon.

So back to the job.

Back at the base we found the group had taken it on the chin from fighters again while we were on pass.[53]

After their leave in London, the reality of the Koltun crew's situation hit heavily.

Bud and the crew returned from their leave to discover that many of their men had been shot down by the German Luftwaffe during a mission in Juvincourt, France. One plane (out of eight) was shot down, and ten men were reported missing in action.

It was just luck or fate that Bud and the Koltun crew were out of the action during that deadly mission.

They were back on it immediately after their return from leave, however, with another mission in France.

Bud records the events here:

June 23

"Bad Cold Makes Me Uncomfortable"

Fifty-two of these pesky 100 pounders again for an airfield near Leon, France. Which airfield is in doubt due to much circling and a second run. Saw a B-24 go down in a lazy spiral—one chute

---

53 Here Bud understates the enormous tragedy of the losses to the 492nd. The group had been part of an all-out Allied effort to "pounce" on Hitler's "Fortress Europe," with D-Day, June 6, 1944, representing a major culmination in the effort. As June wore on, however, the 492nd experienced higher casualties with June 23rd seeing the stunning loss of one of the group's planes, along with the loss of the entire crew. http://www.492ndbombgroup.com/cgi-bin/pagepilot.cgi?page=492history

came out. We had the usual flak holes. Most of the mission was above solid clouds. Rather dull but we hit the target—or some target. Bad cold makes me uncomfortable.

MISSION 11
PERRONE, FRANCE

June 25

"One Engine Was Losing Oil"

Short one to a transformer site at Roye southeast of Ameins. Beautiful day over France but leader took us over flak anyway. One engine was losing oil in the assembly and the nervous engineer saying "You're taking the responsibility, Pilot," wanted to turn back. The even more nervous tail-gunner backed him up. Koltun asked me what I thought and I told him "Hell, it's a short one, men, very short, we can come back on three engines and we don't want to miss an easy one." We kept on though we had to chase the group all the way across the channel and just go into formation as we crossed the enemy coast.

ACTIVE DUTY IN EUROPE

June 27

"As We Were About To Take Off Someone Yelled 'Flak'"

Dear Folks,

Recently we flew a crew to an RAF fighter base south of London to pick up one of our planes that was damaged and had to land there. It was the first British base I'd been on and the visit was thoroughly enjoyed.

The place was permanently situated and had fine brick buildings with every comfort. It was quite collegiate, in fact, with a WAAF[54] contingent giving the co-ed touch.

This was home for several of the famous Spitfire squadrons and we swarmed over the trim little kits, still dressed in our heavy flying suits, discussing their performance with the English mechanics who were very friendly.

A tall, cool, very British "Leftenant"[55] finally took us to tea and we straggled into their spacious officer's lounge looking like quite a bunch of bums but enjoying the change from our crude quarters at the 492nd.

Tiny cheese sandwiches and tea went very well and I hated to leave the place.

Walking to our plane in the bright sunlight we watched two Spitfires hurtle over the ground and climb steeply into the air after an incredibly short run while the wide-open roar of their engines made the air tremble. We kept on walking toward our plane when there was a sharp explosion and looking to the east

---

54 The WAAF was the Women's Auxiliary Air Force, which was the women's auxiliary group of the Royal Air Force. These women served the men of the Royal Air Force by driving, cooking and performing clerical and administration services.
55 "Leftenant," slang for "Lieutenant."

we saw a cloud of black smoke in the air that marked the end of another buzz bomb. The two spitfires frolicked in it enjoying their victory.

As we were about to take off someone yelled "flak" and ahead of us we saw the familiar black puffs, English this time, following along the skyline just behind a tiny plane going at a great speed in a perfect bee-line.

A second later two Spitfires[56] dove on the bug and we saw a flash on its tail as one of the plane's cannon shells hit, but it kept on going until the other plane made a pass and rolled gracefully away. Then the buzz-bomb, sorely hit, dove into the ground and exploded very satisfactorily.

We saw yet another merry chase while taking off. The fighters have done most of the work defending London from these missiles and though it's fun to watch, it's plenty dangerous for the pilots.

From London it was back to Germany and a mission to Saarbrucken.

Bud describes the mission (involving a serious injury to a crew member) in detail here:

---

[56] The Spitfire was a interceptor aircraft capable of a very high top speed. The planes had an elliptical wing design which helped it to reach very high speeds. The Spitfire was the only British plane to stay in production throughout WWII. Source: www.en.wikipedia.org/wiki/Supermarine_Spitfire

MISSION 12
SAARBRUCKEN, GERMANY

June 28

"Bryan's Forehead Was Grey Above His Mask And His Eyes Were Dull."

Hit the marshalling yards at Saarbrucken by radar through the clouds. Despite our efforts to foul up the German radar by dropping aluminum foil[57] while in the target area, their flak was right on us through the clouds.

I had just dropped the bombs and was busy recording figures in my log and trying not to notice the bursts outside when the interphone began to come alive and I heard voices yelling at me "See what's wrong with the nose gunner—Bryan's wounded." My heart almost stood still with fear as I turned around keeping my wires and oxygen tube straightened out and opened the back door in the nose turret. Bryan's forehead was grey above his mask and his eyes were dull. He held up his right hand. The glove on the index finger was cut through and flecked with blood. I couldn't see his finger. He wanted to pull off the glove but I signaled him not to. He started to get out of the turret, now better ventilated than ever by the entrance and exit of the piece of flak.

I shoved him back in the turret with a now wildly pounding heart and sat down to decide what to do. I called the pilot and told him Bryan had almost lost a finger, that it was too cold in

---

[57] The aluminum foil industry went through major growth during World War II, as it was discovered that the product has great utility on the fields of war. It was used as packaging for food and other supplies, but was also found to be very effective as a radar shield in "foil drops," which helped to throw enemy navigation off course. Source: www.aluminumfoils.com.

the nose for him to stay and that he could walk to the main deck carrying a walk-around bottle of oxygen. Then I unstrapped the portable oxygen container from the wall, opened the turret, helped the guy out and shoved him on his way through the tunnel up to the pilot who gave him first aid while Ted flew.

As soon as we'd cleared the enemy coast we left the formation and sped home alone. I gave him a heading for Yarmouth from the Dutch coast and was so pleased when we hit it on the nose that I did not cautiously listen for the call sign of the radio station at our field but merely told the pilot to follow the radio needle on in. I discovered the radio was inoperative in time to do some dead reckoning and pilotage to get home, but I was in a frightful sweat literally for a while. Never again will I trust the radio completely.

The eager radio man fired flares as we circled the field and the ambulance was waiting for our wounded gunner. He was in pain when we landed because he had refused to take morphine while in the enemy's land.

All of our nerves were drawn tight as a drum by this time and Murphy, the sour engineer, set things off by saying to the radio man as the ambulance drove away, "You sure were slow about getting those flares fired, Gilmore," this with a smile. The sensitive Gilmore turned on him with fire in his eyes and for several minutes gave him such a tongue lashing as we have never heard. They never spoke for long months after that except in line of business on the plane. Murphy said he took the insults only because he knew the strain Gilmore was under.

✈

A day later the crew flew back to Madegeburg, Germany, for a bombing raid on an oil refinery...

Here's Bud's telling of those events:

MISSION 13
MADGEBURG, GERMANY

June 29

"Piece of Flak Knocked Me Down"

Carried a load of incendiaries[58] to an aircraft engine plant at Magdeburg in Central Germany. A satisfying mission in the brutal way that is the only way it can be to a bomber crew.

This was a ramrod into the heart of Germany on a beautiful clear day—a bombardier's dream—you could see for 50 miles. The four horsemen[59] were riding with us that day—in every direction as far as you could see smoke palls hung over the enemy's cities. The fatherland[60] was burning.

The sky was filled with the little clusters of specks that marked distant groups and wings of our planes, each with its special target in this area that was being saturated.

Piece of flak knocked me down but was deflected by body armor.

---

58 "Incendiaries" were the bombs (jellied gasoline and explosives inside a metal casing) used to attack military targets during the war.

59 This is a reference to "The Four Horsemen of the Apocalypse," from the Book of Revelation in the last chapter of the New Testament of The Holy Bible. The four horsemen, (symbolizing Pestilence, War, Famine and Death) are seen as signs of the coming apocalypse, or God's final judgement on humanity.

60 The term "Fatherland" was used frequently during the time of Nazi Germany, as it referred to the great power instilled in the German government at that time. The German love of rules and order seemed to find reassurance in the notion of a great "father" who would act as caretaker for the German people. Source: www.reference.com/geography/germany-called-fatherland

Over, under, ahead and behind swung quartets of our fighters—moving gracefully across us or peeling off in sudden diving turns when they sensed trouble.

I often stand up in the plexiglass dome on top of my compartment and look around at the formation bobbing up and down on all sides or back at the pilot's cockpit where two monstrous creatures with green eyes (sun goggles), grey rubber faces and 10 foot nose tubes stare unblinkingly back.

This precision bombing is a wonderful thing when the weather is good and the bombardier has half a chance—one little factory area out of a city and the rest untouched. We've seen cities the RAF has ruined and I like our way. They can plaster the whole city at night and easily miss vital plants. I don't see how they can have any moral ground to stand on in complaining of these unaimed buzz bombs except, of course, that the Germans started mass bombings of cities.

✈

June 30

"I Was Quite Thoroughly Drenched"

Dear Folks,

Whenever possible I ride my girls' bike through the country. It restores a little of the balance and never fails to brighten me up.

Summer has finally started to come and the sky is often filled with towering cumulus clouds.

I rode beyond the village and paused on a hilltop to watch the sun set behind some black thunderheads. Turning up a farmer's road I noticed some cottontail rabbits playing in the path with complete trust. The wind was down, the only sounds was the cawing of some crows. Grey clouds started to move over, hastening the coming of night.

Coming home along the darkening road, listening to the rustling murmur of the wind in the great old trees by the roadside brought back memories of many summer nights on the sleeping porch. There's no sound quite so soothing.

Because I dreamed along so slowly a cloudburst, one of those things I thot didn't happen here, caught me in the dark ¼ mile from home and I was quite thoroughly drenched.

Well, I was given the air medal recently for completing a certain number of missions (5). It's a nice medal but means nothing and the extravagant language of the citation that goes with it disgusts me. We call it the 8th AAF good conduct medal cause all fliers have one just as all ground men have a good conduct medal.

One medal was given that made us all sit up and take notice at an extremely dull ceremony. The DFC[61] was handed to old Bridges, the Texan I rode with once. On a mission before we arrived here he had two engines stopped, a main wing spar shot through and a rudder shot in half by fighters yet he kept the plane under control, continued to the target, bombed and brought it back—at the same time fighting a fire. Just about any-

---

61 The Distinguished Flying Cross, which was medal given out for "heroism or extraordinary achievement while participating in an aerial flight, subsequent to November 11, 1918." This DSC is the second highest award given out by the US Army.— Source: Wikipedia www.wikipedia.org/wiki/Distinguished_Service_Cross_(United_States)

one else would have jumped, but this guy decided to sweat it out and got away with it.

You see the trouble—they have no sense about these awards—they give medals so promiscuously that when a man really deserves some recognition, a medal doesn't give it.

✈

5 July, 1944

"The Gunners Just Have To Sit And Wait The Weary, Anxious Hours Out"

Dear Folks,

I have your letter, Pa, asking me to let the chips fall where they may in telling of the missions. You've received some sort of description of the first ones—I really can't remember what I did or didn't say.

Flak is fascinating to watch even though I find it easier on my nerves if I don't. I remember looking out the window sort of absently at a space of blue sky when in an instant four shells burst magically where I watched. Bright flashes of red in the center with black oily smoke on the outside. Only the smoke remains drifting quickly by.

We navigators have an ideal job as far as nervous tension goes. We're almost continually at work when on a mission, checking the position, telling the pilot when he can expect the formation to turn so that he will be ready for it when it comes and won't struggle, giving the crew oxygen checks (each position reports to be sure no one is k.o'd by anoxia[62].) We also give the crew approximate positions "20 miles south of Paris" etc., and tell the gunners when to expect our fighters to pick us up. All this activity, though fatiguing, keeps our minds comparatively free from brooding and we can look at a German city with glee, "Hooray, a check-point, I am no longer lost."

The gunners just have to sit and wait the weary, anxious hours out—listening to me monopolize the interphone reports of progress, items of interest about the topography below us, and any jokes I can think of.

On the bombing run, the most critical and exciting part, I'm bombardier or chief button pusher and am preoccupied with other things beside the flak which of late I have seen little of because I'm squatting on the floor and can only see down. Lately you see we've been flying in a position above the leader.

Over the target, especially in Germany, we expect flak and always get it. The tension starts to mount 10 minutes or so before the target as we ride along with the bomb doors open and all switches on. We see the shells breaking up ahead and then are in their midst—that's the worst part, seeing it up ahead and knowing you'll be in it in a minute.

I have time estimated for us to be at the target and keep calling out how many minutes to go as we approach.

When pieces from a shell hit the plane it sounds like tin cans being slapped together. Immediately the pilot or I have each position report any casualties or damage.

---

[62] Anoxia is a condition that occurs when an inadequate oxygen supply is provided to an organ's tissues, even though there is enough blood being delivered. This condition can be brought on by smoke or inhalation of carbon monoxide, or due to high altitude exposure (as in a plane flying at high altitudes). In severe cases a person with anoxia may become comatose or experience seizures. Source: www.neuroskills.com/brain-injury/anoxia-and-hypoxia.php

Lately on the bombing run when we see it hot and heavy ahead I've been singing into the interphone "Here we go again, I hear that trumpet blow again."[63]

Then there's the RAF joke I've used many times at similar moments, never with much success though. As the sky begins to explode I say with British solemnity, "Hmm, natives appear unfriendly."

On the ground when you know you're to fly again soon it's amazing how you exaggerate to yourself the perils. In the air it's never as bad as imagined. I've found, as many men have, that the way to conquer fear is to face it, examine it, realize its basis. Such an attitude does stop some of the worrying, anyway.

As a result, I expect to be shot down every time I go up and as always sure to have my escape kit (to aid evasion in enemy countries) and parachute where I can get at them. Koltun is amazed by such an attitude—he says he just knows everything will be all right and seldom worries.

Such is the difference between men, he never knows where his chute is and I've seen him sleeping above Germany while Dagood flew.

When we are finally back safe on the ground again I am always in unusually good spirits because I've been granted a respite from expected disaster. I rush from the plane to the truck with my gear in hand shouting "Hey, hey, we're back, we're safe, we're still alive, ain't it wonderful, men?" After the interrogation on a long mission we are often given a pint of Scotch to divide among the crew and half a glass of that on a stomach that has been empty for nine hours really makes me happy.

---

63 From the song, "Taking a Chance on Love," which was published in 1940 and recorded by numerous vocal legends of the era (and after), including Frank Sinatra, Ethel Waters, Ella Fitzgerald, Tony Bennett and more. The song was composed by Vernon Duke with lyrics by John La Touche and Ted Fetter.

Chattering loudly we stroll back to the huts, chewing on grass stems and singing together—"Boy, and nothing to do till the next one."

✈

After a brief break the boys were back in the air, this time on a mission to Kiel, Germany, and with a submarine base in their sites.
Here's Bud's view of the raid:

MISSION 14
KIEL, GERMANY

July 6

"I'm Afraid The Crew Is A Little Suspicious
That It is My Fault"

Load of incendiaries and general purpose bombs for Keil, Germany. I dreaded the mission and the 140 guns they told us about at the target. Our group led the 8th AAF. Clear weather except over the target. Half our bombs hung up (wouldn't drop) and the piles finally got them out with the emergency release. Maintenance of our bombing equipment is terrible and worries the crew. They hate to have those incendiaries get stuck since a flak hole in one of them could be unpleasant. I'm afraid the crew is a little suspicious that it is my fault partly that the bomb releasing seems to be fouled up half the time, but I have a check list system and know that I've done everything I should have.

✈

Bud's record of the war also includes insights recorded in a personal diary, which he passed on to his mother after the war. The diary entries help piece together the events that ensued between his letters home.

As Bud writes:

Diary

"The Figures Looked Very Much Alive"

Had another pass to London and read in the papers about the 8th AAF losing 30 bombers to fighters. When we got back, we found out that our group had lost 15 of the 30 including three of the five crews we came from Westover with. Morale isn't very good and our bombing record is worse.

In London we saw Mme. Tussaud's[64] waxworks.

I spent a fascinated hour strolling through her vast establishment looking at extremely life-like wax figures of everyone from Hitler to the first English King. The figures looked very much alive but in many cases bore only superficial likeness to the person represented. Very human though, especially the eyes. They were so good I'd catch myself feeling self-conscious when standing in front of a staring group. All those household names standing before me in facsimile, only men like other men after all.

I visited catholic Westminster Cathedral, still under construction though started 50 years ago. Instead of the usual Gothic, it is Byzantine and quite eastern. Built of brick but the inside

---

64 Madame Tussaud's historic wax museum was established in London in 1836 and is still attracting crowds to its eerily realistic wax figures today. Bud's fascination with wax museums may have begun during the war, but it remained a life-long (and oddball) area of interest throughout his life (as his children, who accompanied him to numerous wax museums in various locales from Honolulu to San Francisco to Anaheim can attest).

is slowly being faced with polished, highly grained marble and stone mosaics, very expertly done.

From the cathedral tower 300 feet high I get an excellent view of mid-afternoon London. The dome of St. Paul's is the most prominent mark in the sky.

Strolling around the big stores I was impressed by the way the English clerks go about selling you—they don't—they just let you talk yourself into it with no high pressure.

Back at the base Tres (who couldn't go with us) greeted the crew with a basket of huge red strawberries he'd wangled off some farm woman for ony 50 cents. Plenty sweet without sugar.

Koltun's portable radio is still with us after all the travels and we hear a lot of music, most of it from Germany.

✈

The other day our crew was assigned to test flight a plane after an engine change. We had a lot of fun by having the co-pilot navigate and me fly. We'd ask him what a certain town was and he, imitating me, would hem and haw and complain of the forecast wind and finally come up with the obvious answer.

I flew the plane for an hour and landed it almost all alone, Koltun said. It took all my strength to hold that wheel back as we touched the ground.

✈

As Bud mentions, the 492nd Bomb Group sustained heavy casualties while the Koltun crew was on leave. They returned to find, again, that many of the men in their unit had been killed while they were relaxing in London. Once again, due to the strange "luck" of war, they survived while their mates succumbed.

There was little time then to dwell on these devastating events, however, as the boys were back on another mission within days, this time, to Munich.

Here's Bud's description of the dramatic mission over Munich:

MISSION 15
MUNICH, GERMANY

July 12

"Just A Long, Long Haul"

Incendiaries and explosives dumped in the center of Munich, Germany's center of culture.

Bombing by radar—overcast all the way. Just a long, long haul—9 hours of it.

ABORTION

July 13

"The Electric Releases Worked Fine This Time"

Couldn't get our wheels retracted and fog moved in on the field so we flew out again into the North Sea. Took radio fixes and tried to dump the bombs near where the ground told us to. Of course, the electric releases worked fine this time. We landed at Hanston, east of London, a big crash field and had the landing gear repaired.

✈

MISSION 16
SAARBRUCKEN, GERMANY

July 15

"Find Myself Still Quite Fearful Of The Flak."

Another dull mission above the overcast to Saarbrucken's railroad yards. Nothing so tiresome as looking at that solid white layer of clouds below us. Bombs went electrically in good shape for a change. No flak holes in the ship for the second time in a row. Find myself still quite fearful of the flak.

July 16

"We Are Not A Lead Crew And Have Very Little Chance Of Ever Becoming One"

Dear Folks,

Every night after supper we drift by our bulletin board and after a moment's hesitation run our eyes down the list of crews who will fly the next morning. Most of the time we see our crew there—"Oh well, what the hell"—shrug the shoulders with a sigh and go on to our hut and a bull session or a book.

The nicest thing that happens to us is to be on the list for tomorrow's mission and going to sleep with that in mind to waken in the morning, look at the watch and see that the mission must have been scrubbed (cancelled) and go back to sweet sleep till noon—what luxury, what thankfulness.

We are not a lead crew and have very little chance of ever becoming one as we were replacements to this group which naturally had its lead crews already selected and trained. I'm torn between being glad and sad about it—a position of terrifying responsibility for the navigator and yet a chance for immense gratification if you are successful. I've seen murder in the faces of our gunners when some lead navigator took us over a flak field by mistake.

✈

Last night I took a bike ride on a different road and discovered a magnificent old forest—ancient gnarled trees by the narrow road making a green tunnel a million miles from anywhere.

I stopped a moment and sitting on a giant root munched a candy bar, almost forgetting about the war

MISSION 17
CAEN, FRANCE

July 18

"All We Could See From 20,000 Was Dust"

Salvoed a load of 100 pounders on a big area five miles east of Caen on the Normandy beachhead[65]. Toggle switch didn't work and this time I know why—I didn't have the pointer turned up—first time I've known what went wrong—fortunate-

---

65 The Normandy beachhead (comprised of four beaches: Omaha, Utah, Gold and Juno Beach) was the entry point for the Allied forces on "D-Day," June 6, 1944, when the American, British and Canadian forces stormed the beaches as part of "Operation Overlord," which turned the course of the war over that summer. By August 1944 Paris was liberated from the Nazis and the German forces' surrender followed in April of 1945.

ly didn't matter much this time. We saw just a pall of smoke where the British were trying to break out of the position they've been checked in at Caen. All we could see from 20,000 was dust occasionally lit up by a bright flash.

✈

From Caen it was on to Germany again after a short break.
Here Bud records his observations of the dramatic mission over Oberpfaffenhofen Field, in another letter to his mother and father:

MISSION 18
OBERPFAFFENHOFEN, GERMANY

July 21

"Ten Bombs Didn't Fall"

Incendiaries for an airport west of Munich. Very tense, tiring ride dodging in and out of clouds and contrails (clouds formed by planes).

Approaching the target the tail gunner saw a B-24 in the group behind us go down on fire from a sneak fighter attack.

Co-pilot saw another bomber blow up off to our right from a stray flak shot. Thus we were a bit keyed up by the time we were on the bombing run. Target was clear. Having no trust in the electric release system, I again dropped manually by moving the big salvo lever when I saw the leader drop. Things instantly became confused—the radio man called on the interphone "10 bombs didn't fall"—the plane went into a steep dive way out of formation for the 10 bombs had all piled up on the bottom layer in the bomb bay and spilling out sideways they had tangled the control wires that run along the bomb bay wall. The pilot and co-pilot fought the controls trying to get the ship under control, at the same time the gunners in the waist rushed to the bomb bay and with commendable speed loosened the bombs that were jamming the controls.

We struggled back to formation still carrying the 10 incendiaries. 100 pounders full of jellied gasoline and rubber. We worked for an hour on the way home trying to get the tangled mass of bombs and wires out of the plane but to no avail. They just wouldn't drop. I crawled back in the bomb bay with a portable oxygen bottle but felt more helpless than anybody.

We couldn't land in England with a mess like that but how could we get rid of them? Then someone suggested trying the electric release system—we'd tried everything else—it didn't seem logical that it would work when the big salvo bar hadn't but we agreed to try and opened the bomb bay doors.

We were over a German forest at the time and when everything was all set up I flicked the toggle switch and the ten troublemakers tumbled down and started a forest fire below us. We don't know how bad a one it developed but the smoke was starting to pour up as we passed on.

After this run of missions, the boys were overdue for a rest. They were granted a leave and took the opportunity to travel and sight-see while they rejuvenated from an exhausting series of flights.

Bud ventured off to Scotland on his own, his natural curiosity and passion still unflagging, even with the weight of the war bearing down on him and his crew.

TRIP TO SCOTLAND

July 29

"Wanted To See Scotland But Had To Go Alone"

Dear Folks,

Quite a leave we just had, six days of freedom with all of the United Kingdom to ramble about in and no other object but to entertain ourselves.

Wanted to see Scotland but had to go alone cause Tres couldn't get leave and the pilots liked London so well they didn't relish a long train ride to a town that might not be as good.

The trains in England are twice as crowded as any in the states and so slow that traveling very far requires the patience of Job[66]. On the way to Scotland I was jammed in passageways with soldiers, sailors and RAF of both sexes, even civilians, and though everyone was very good natured and tolerant of the jostling, it was a dreary trip. I managed to read "The Tales of De Maupassant"[67] leaning on a window (your old red volume that somehow never was burned at home.)

Edinburgh is a beautiful city and surpasses London by far in planning. The streets are fine and wide with all the imposing vistas I've looked for in London.

---

66 Job is the biblical figure who endured incredible hardships and tragedies only to be blessed by God later in life. The book of James in the King James version of the new Testament of the Holy Bible refers to "the patience of Job." Source: www.bibleodyssey.org

67 The "Tales of De Maupassant" was a famous collection of stories by the French writer (1850-1893) Guy De Maupassant, who was considered a master of the fictional short story form.

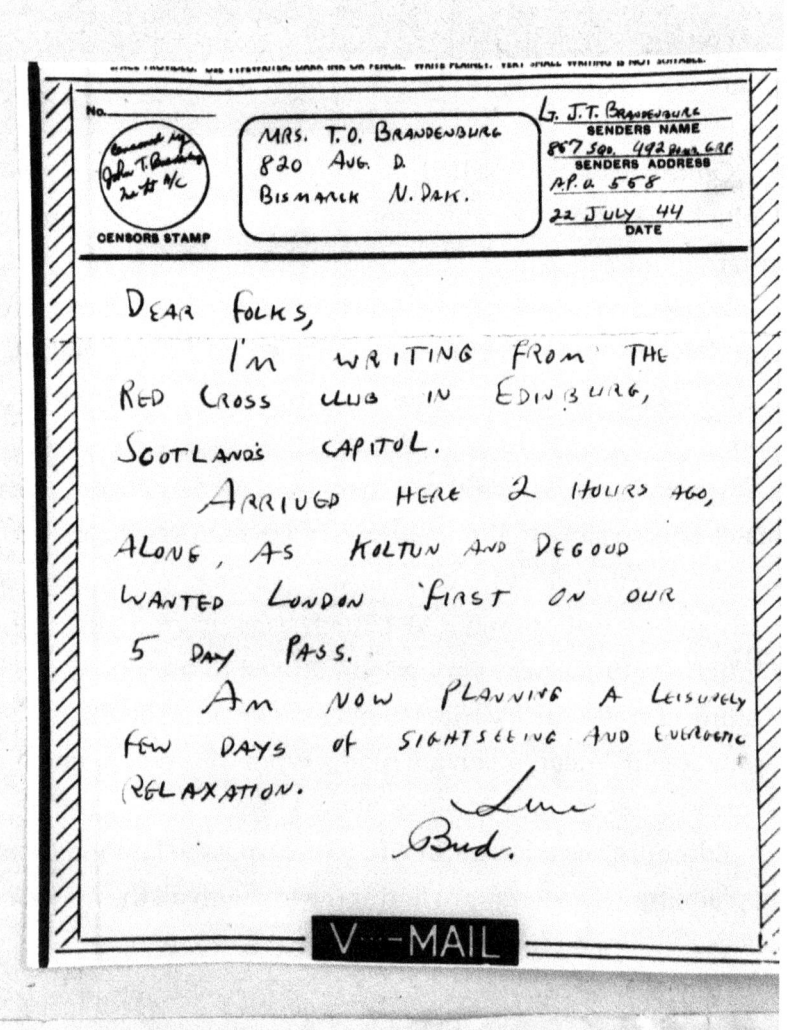

Hand-written note home from Edinburgh, Scotland.

The principal street is Princess, a straight, broad avenue through the center of town with a lovely park paralleling it for many blocks. From the park the formidable old castle on its great rock is in fine view and only a ten-minute walk away.

On the edge of this park are several classic Greek structures, art museums, and beside them every night soapbox orators gather their crowds.

I got a kick out of listening to them because the audience participates and there is a lot of heckling. Main topics seemed to be the usual religious revivals, Catholic baiting and communism (the "capitalist's war), though a few were trying to start a crusade to "get the Scotsman's land away from the English overseer."

There was one old lawyer wearing his courtroom cloak who just stood and talked, letting his mind run free, saying anything that came to him. He had a big crowd and was quite amusing, getting a lot of laughs from his pokes at the English—a favorite pastime up there, we found.

He stood with his hands on his hips—"Now in London they're taking it again (buzz bombs)—yes, yes taking it—wonderful people—standing up to it again—I ask you what else can they do" and he laughs. He was a bit cracked and admitted it saying he was a better man than the rest of his family since they were all lunatics, but he alone knew it.

Listening to the woman communist go to town, I got in a discussion with a middle-aged lady and a Scotch gentleman. Scoring a point, I got a bravo from a cute WAAF beside me (female of the RAF species.) She turned out to be a Russian and thus began a short but enjoyable friendship.

I took her walking up to the castle and monument inspecting until it was dark. She was a resident of Moscow—communist party member—educated in Germany—spoke French and English besides German and Russian. I had to speak more slowly than usual so she could understand.

This Russian was a lot like an American girl—hearty, happy, unrestrained, though less bushbeating and more straight from the shoulder talking.

She is here with 25 comrades working in London interrogating Luftwaffe prisoners—every 14 months she gets back to Russia.

Sunday, I attended St. Giles Cathedral for the morning service and was well content with the program.

The choir was completely in feeling with its majestic setting and the sermon by the presbyter was sensible and undogmatic. "Lift up your eyes unto the hill" he said and continually referred to Arthur's Seat, a great rock bluff above town, in analogues concerning the strength of faith.

The cathedral is an old Norman one (or so I took it to be) without the slender gracefulness of the English gothic but still very nice. The Gothic is much better for the audience as they don't have to crane their heads around the massive pillars of the Norman—but I had an excellent seat so the pillars didn't matter.

This is the official worship spot for the King and Queen when in Scotland and there is a special division for them and their party away from the commoners.

In the afternoon I took a walking tour sponsored by the Red Cross and in a motley crowd of paratroopers from Normandy, Glider pilots, Navy ensigns, etc. We walked down to Holyrood

ACTIVE DUTY IN EUROPE

palace, their majesty's official residence in Scotland and the site of the tragic doings in the unhappy life of Mary Queen of Scots[68].

At the palace, one wing of which dates from 1498, we joined a crowd of civilians of all descriptions and jostled our way under the firm but benevolent hand of a crisp old Scottish guide through the many chambers of the place. Mary of Scotland's room—her bed—her secret stairway to the chapel where she meditated—we gaped at it all.

The old guide showed us a bronze plaque in the floor—"The very spot where Rizzio, Mary's secretary, fell punctured by 53 dagger wounds." The old fellow then told us in the singsong developed by all guides that there used to be no plaque on the floor and the caretakers of the place would mark the spot with red paint. However, he said, people were always scraping away parts of the floor with the red on it and carrying it to far countries calling it a bit of Rizzio's blood which was all right, he said, only hard on the floor, so being a good Scotsman, he had the tablet installed.

Walking back to the slub up the "Royal Mile," we passed John Knox's house and noted the window from which he used to harangue the multitudes.

Later on, dosing on the grass in the park, I noticed a girl take a park bench nearby.

I rose to go and she stopped me though she was very embarrassed and said so. She said that she had been sent to meet a friend here to take home to tea with her mother. The friend hadn't come, she didn't want to disappoint her old mother,

---

68 Mary, Queen of Scots (who was also known as Mary Stuart) served as the Queen of Scotland from 1542 until 1567. Her father (who died while she was an infant) was King James V of Scotland. She was found guilty of plotting to assassinate her cousin, Queen Elizabeth I of England, and was beheaded after spending 18 1/2 years in Elizabeth's custody in various English castles.

would I come? She was young and innocent looking, seemed actually embarrassed; I had nothing to do and as a result, off we went.

On the trolley she asked if I hadn't been embarrassed. "No," I said, laughing, "I've been in London too much."

Her mother was a hunched up little old lady with sparkling eyes who became quite friendly after the preliminary coldness was gone, telling of her daughters and their troubles, of her 20 years in China, Shanghai and Hong Kong, etc. Really a talented family; her husband was a trader in Shanghai—she wanted to go back to China, went there as a bride, thought it was the only country.

She showed me her treasures—silverware, silver fruit stands and mirrors from china all with the imperial dragon crawling around the handles. Really lovely things.

It was rather a nice afternoon; we had tea and Scottish scones and all manner of delicacies before I left. Must write the good woman a thank you note.

She was not Mrs. Cranna's type of warm hearted. Once I got her going I couldn't get a word in and surprisingly enough they learned little of me while I learned all about them. The fact that her young daughter is not in school but is taking care of her, also pointed to a selfish nature, but I shall not look gift mothers in the teeth or cooking or wherever you look.

The next day I discovered myself getting quite jumpy just relaxing, probably cause I knew no one and things were a bit too quiet, so I hied myself to the airport, waiting around with a paratrooper who told me of D-Day, and hooked an army transport going south.

On board was a tall distinguished looking civilian who seemed rather lost, and I was friendly so we had tea in the Midlands together waiting for a train after our plane landed. He was an ex-Russian czarist cavalry officer, and we had a nice chat.

The buzz bombs[69] in London were almost negligible so after I met the lads at our officer's club, I decided to stay, and we had a rather good time during the rest of the week just taking it easy, sleeping on clean sheets, going to shows and amusing ourselves.

Chester Barefoot[70], an Oklahoman and electrical engineer has become a good friend; he's a navigator on another crew from Westover. Bucktoothed and red-faced, he still has a sly charm and wester air that in his quiet way has made him a valuable companion.

We're flying again and shall continue for quite a while yet. The outfit we are in has a minimum of 30 missions required before we are taken out of combat. It's in sight but will take quite a while yet.

---

69 The "buzz bombs" were V-1 flying bombs, (also called doodlebugs) which were early pulse-jet powered cruise missiles. These bombs were directed at London, in bombing raids that began just one week after D-Day, on June 13, 1944. The buzz bombings of England by Germany continued until the Allied Forces shut down all of the launch facilities in October of 1944.
70 Chester Barefoot was a native American 8AAF crew member who became a close friend of Bud during their service in the 492nd bomb group They shared great camaraderie during their service together and Bud mourned Chester's untimely death (in combat) greatly. In his later years Bud wept openly when speaking of "my old pal, Chester Barefoot."

Chapter 3

Breakup of the 492nd Bomb Group

Bud's adventures on leave in England and Scotland provided a well-needed break in the action, and yet on the crew's return to active duty they were greeted with disconcerting news regarding their assignment with the 492nd Bomb Group.

Here the crew's Log Book (see Log Book section at the end of Bud's letters) marks this significant event; the breakup of the 492nd Bomb Group. Though the date noted is August 22nd, 1944, the announcement must have come at the end of July. The group was officially disbanded on August 8, 1944, after just 89 days of active duty. According to the website, www.492ndbombgroup.com, the group was the only combat group in US history to have been disbanded.

While the bomb group itself was separated, the Koltun crew was left mostly intact, and moved into the 445th Bomb Group. The group gained more notoriety in recent years as it became known that actor James Stewart ("It's a Wonderful Life," "Vertigo") acted as commanding officer over all four squadrons in the 445th in 1944-45 (a fact Bud never mentioned to his family).

Given the original 492nd's harrowing record of casualties (80% of the men serving in the group were lost to attacks by the Luftwaffe), the government may have felt great urgency in breaking up the group.

BREAKUP OF THE 492ND BOMB GROUP

Ultimately, there were two "492nd" bomb groups. The original 492nd Bomb Group flew daytime missions out of the airfield at North Pickenham, England, up until August 8, 1944. After that time, another bomb group, the 801st, (nicknamed "The Carpetbaggers") became the 492nd Bomb Group, on August 13, 1944. The Carpetbaggers continued flying nighttime, covert missions under the new designation of the 492nd Bomb Group from that time on.

And so, on August 8, 1944, the original 492nd Bomb Group was disbanded, and the surviving members of the group were transferred into other bombing groups within the 8th Allied Air Force Army Air Corps.

Here Bud continues his record of the missions, even as the crew was beginning training with the 445th. Bud and the crew kept their history with the 492nd close to the vest as they started their service with the much less experienced crews of the 445th, only revealing their harrowing history after the completion of their 30th mission in the fall of 1944.

MISSION 19
BREMEN, GERMANY

July 29

"Visibility Was Less Than Half A Mile"

Above solid clouds we bombed Bremen by radar with very good results we learned later. Subsequent photos showed we sunk some destroyers in the harbor besides hitting a refinery and the oil storage tanks that were the primary objective.

Heavy flak at the target and Koltun got a scare when a flak piece shattered his side window and scattered glass on him. He has been showing signs of nerves like the rest of us lately and never sleeps on a mission any more.

Trying to land at the fog bound field when we returned was worse than the flak. The engineer and I stood behind the pilots helping them look for planes. Visibility was less than half a mile and the fog was full of planes trying to get in just as we were.

A couple of colonels stood on the end of the runway and fired flares continuously out of ivory pistols to try to help us in.

Koltun just couldn't get lined up with the misty runway in time to get us in on it and we made four passes before finally touching down with such a loud sign from the crew that bystanders must have thought a tire had gone flat.

✈

From Bremen it was on to France again, with a mission to Leon.
Bud writes:

MISSION 20
LAON, FRANCE

August 1

"Radar Bombing Is Not Yet Very Precise"

Carried eight 1000 pounders to Leon France above the overcast and then brought them all back since the target was covered and we are not allowed to bomb in France unless we can see the target. Radar bombing is not yet very precise.

I worked hard with the Gee box (electronic navigational aid) and did o.k.

✈

After Laon, the missions continued full-on, with the crew taking to the air with few breaks in between.

Here's Bud's telling of the dramatic flight of August 3rd, in his letter home.

MISSION 21
MERY SUR OISE, FRANCE

August 3

"Just After "Bombs Away" There Was A Loud Crash"

Bombed a robot bomb supply dump 12 miles north west of Paris. Accurate and intense flak on a long bombing run that put many holes in the ship.

Just after "bombs away" there was a loud crash from the pilot's deck and I heard the radio man scream over the interphone "get the co-pilot!" I called "what's going on, is someone hurt?" Pilot yelled "shut up, we're busy."

An ammunition box used as a seat by the commander in the lead ship just ahead of us had fallen out of the open bomb bay and struck Dagood's window, just grazed his forehead leaving him dazed and bleeding. The box continued on into the bomb bay where it still was when we landed.

Dagood said he vaguely remembered a black object flying toward him and that it was a flak shell. The blow on his head and the blood pouring into his eye made him lose his reason and he sprang from his seat and would have leaped out the bomb bay without a chute if the radio man hadn't caught him and talked some sense into his rattled brain. He thought the plane was crashing.

The radio man made him as comfortable as possible and then tried to help the pilot who was freezing in the -20 degree, 200 mile an hour wind whipping through the shattered co-pilot's window.

When we reached the enemy coast we dove out of formation and high-tailed it for home alone.

I managed to work myself into a sweat navigating because I mistook one English town for another that looked like it but we got in with only a minute of extra flying because I had enough sense to turn the radio compass on. Though the interphone was out I stood up in the bubble[71] on top and pointed the way to the pilot that the radio had shown me. We were within 10 miles of the field but couldn't see it at the time because of haze.

Luckily the co-pilot's wounds were minor and he was flying in three days with four stitches in his forehead.

---

71 "The bubble" Bud refers to was likely the plexiglass nose turret located behind the pilot on top of the bomber.

Undated

"The Time Wore On With Everyone Relaxing As Best They Could"

Dear Folks,

Harvest time is coming over here and field just across the way is covered with shocks. It seems like only a few weeks ago it was covered with sprouting grass.

I walked out tonight and shucked a few heads of wheat—always did like to crunch away on some wheat while harvesting. This stuff was soft though and had no crunch to it. The heads were long and well-filled; a little sunlight now and they ought to get a good yield.

I don't think it's been mentioned but we have class one or two hours every day we're not flying—aircraft identification, etc., held in our maps of every front and racks full of special intelligence magazines—most secret—give us the real uncensored dope on the war.

On the wall every day is hung a long teletyped sheet containing special reports from headquarters on missions—results—losses—opposition. When we bomb thru the clouds this is how we learn if we hit anything or not. On a clear day we can usually see how well we're doing and in addition about every other plane has a camera synchronized with the bomb release that gives the true story to intelligence.

The complexity and efficiency of this air force with its millions of cogs spinning away together for the common purpose continues to amaze me.

Recently one of the crews in our squadron took off on its 30th mission. If they got back today, they'll be first in the group to finish a tour[72].

The mission was due to return in mid-afternoon and all classes and previous engagements were skipped with permission so we could be on hand to join the celebration when the crew landed. Koltun's men weren't flying so we joined the crowd at the plane's parking area to "sweat it out" like the mechanics always do for us.

The ceiling was at 500 feet with the sky covered by dirty gray clouds and a haze restricting visibility to two miles (usual English weather.)

The crowd was composed of everyone from mechanics to a general waiting to pin medals on the lads. Ruth Christianson Register was around in her Red Cross outfit for that last touch.

The time wore on with everyone relaxing as best they could—sitting on bomb carriers, gas drums or anything else handy. A few looies[73] tried to keep Ruth amused by sticking straws in her ears thus amusing a lot of other looies who were watching. One of men's most interesting pastimes is watching other men amusing girls. Maybe it's to pick up pointers in techniques—anyhow Ruth was not too much entertained. She's a pretty, poised kid—you have to be with these air force wolves.

So we waited and pretty soon two or three at a time our planes straggled back down through the overcast. If it's clear, we come over the field in formation and peel off to land but in bad weather we come back singly.

---

72 During 1944 the set tour of duty for crew members flying heavy bombers was 25-30 completed missions.
73 Looies, military slang for "lieutenants."

Everyone watched the landings and commented to neighbors on whether they were good or bad and a looie with some field glasses kept scanning the planes in the air to find the one we were sweating.

B-24's that had landed taxied by on the perimeter track—engines roaring up and then dying as the pilots held the big ships straight down the road with the throttles. Each plane had its man sticking out of the top hatch—greasy, tired faces of engineers or navigators helping the pilot taxi. When a crew would go by that somebody knew there would come great sarcastic cheers and much hand waving.

When Bridge's crew in "The Sweat Box" went by the cheering was a little subdued and genuine for they are the hero crew of the field, having returned twice when it was considered impossible.

I always feel a little emotional seeing the B-24s taxi to their parking place at the end of a mission. Maybe because they sit level on the ground and look like they're still flying. It's probably because I'm still a little romantic and think it's wonderful that these men were over an enemy city four hours ago hundreds of miles away and are now home again.

Just like in the movies the plane we were looking for came into sight last—cautiously buzzed the field once—fired all his flares and came in to land.

As soon as the props stopped turning we crowded around the plane yelling congratulations to the pilots who grinned down on us.

They finally got the crew lined up outside still in their flying togs and took pictures—then the general handed out the DFCs.

In the meantime the lads had been putting the pressure on Ruth and she ran out into the grimy circle of faces and gave all 10 of the crew a real warrior's welcome home by giving them a memorable kiss.

All the fuss over this one crew is not the usual thing—it just happened that they were the first of the originals to finish.

As the crew approached the end of its service with the 492nd, the "hard luck" of the group continued, yet once again the boys of the Koltun crew were miraculously left unscathed, as Bud describes it in this letter home from August of 1944.

✈

MISSION 22
HAMBURG, GERMANY

August 6

"We Ground On With Bomb Bays Open"

Target was an oil refinery at Hamburg, but we only came within nine miles of it. Clear, shining day above Germany.

Our formation crossed north of the city and did a loop around it approaching to bomb from the southwest.

As we paralleled the broad Elbe on the way in the ruined port looked gray—probably because so much is in ashes[74].

---

74 Bud here refers to the port on the Elbe River in Hamburg, which was "in ashes." The port was in Hamburg, which had been subjected to a major bombing raid during the last week of July 1943. The area was targeted as it was an industrial center with oil

Evidently the jerries thought there was still something of value in the place, though, for the sky was very heavily speckled with black dots of old and new flak burst and I sighed at the sight—pulled my GI helmet down closer and rearranged the extra flak suits on the floor to cover a greater area.

We ground on with bomb bays open now and I called out "four minutes to the target" which meant that in about one minute we'd be in flak range.

It was just about time to be saying "here we go again" when one engine choked and lost power so badly the pilot called "feather number two" (turn prop blades so they offer no resistance to the air while not running). A second later another engine began to whine and roar louder and louder while the plane swerved violently—we couldn't hold our place in the formation—we only had three engines now and another was running away (revolutions per minute governor was out).

We dropped back out of our formation but the tail gunner called that the group behind us would soon run us down or go over us which is just as bad on a bombing run when the bombs start falling. We had been listening to all these excited announcements on the interphone—they had only taken a few seconds—and were not surprised when the pilot called "Brandy, salvo the bombs—we've got to get out of the way of the group following us."

---

refineries. The bombings unexpectedly created a massive firestorm which destroyed most of the city and took thousands of civilian lives.

    Novelist Kurt Vonnegut served in the Allied army in Europe at the time, and was captured during the Battle of the Bulge and taken to Dresden, another city that endured heavy bombing and mass destruction by the Allied Forces during the war (in February of 1945). Vonnegut wrote of his experience as a survivor of the firestorm in his anti-war novel, "Slaughterhouse Five." Source: www.wikipedia.org/wiki/Bombing (of Hamburg in World War II).

I grabbed the big lever, released the safety catch and shoved with considerable eagerness. The plane jumped with relief as the big 500 pounders fell away.

Unfortunately there was a little village just ahead of us about 9 miles from the outskirts of Hamburg. The bombs seemed to be falling directly toward it as I watched from the bottom window. It was hardly a time for philosophic speculation but I hated to see the bombs heading for that village and was vastly relieved when they burst in a field several hundred yards beyond.

The hurried exertion of salvoing the bombs had disconnected my interphone microphone wire and now while I hunted frantically for the loose end of the wire I could hear the pilots arguing which way to turn now that we were out of the path of the bombers behind us. They continually tried to call me but getting no answer—I was taking them north east of Hamburg, a bad decision since the idea was to get home without being shot at.

I finally got the wire connected and got us turned back to the west just over the outskirts of town and just out of flak range. We weren't shot at anyway—perhaps the defenders were too busy now with our comrades whom we could see sailing through the heavy flak and plowing up the town with their bombs.

The runaway engine was now under control but we still had only three and couldn't stay with the formation when we met them (by cutting corners) as they came off the target.

By this time we were feeling pretty good since I had us on the flak-free briefed route home though there were great naval bases on each side of the course just out of range. Once the pilot asked me if I was sure we'd get no flak coming out this way since he saw a formation to the left going in the same direction. I told him I knew we were coming out the way we should and was confirmed the next minute when the formation to our left ran into those ugly little puffs over Wesermunde.

There had been a radio call to be alert for enemy fighters in the vicinity but none had shown up and we could see the North Sea ahead of us.

We continued on alone out over the water in fine spirits. The little island of Helegoland[75] took one shot at us "just to show us they're awake" as a gunner said, but it burst ¼ of a mile away.

The engines held up and we came home without any trouble.

The rest of the crew was already in the truck while I was still gathering up my maps and putting things in order in my spot in the plane when I saw out the side window the silver tail of a B-24 sticking up through a cloud of dust and then settling back. Then I saw men running all at once and heard shouts of "crash!"

I slipped out the nose-wheel door as fast as I could and ran to the truck. Someone said "Two of our planes just collided as they came in to land." We looked ahead with a mixture of horror and curiosity at the pillar of smoke rising from the end of the runway.

The truck with our crew took a road that led right by the two wrecks and we sat in tense silence as we went by. A big crowd had gathered around the scattered piles of metal and men. Five men were taken out alive from one plane but all were lost in the burning one and ammunition was popping in it while we wound slowly by.

We cursed the truck driver for taking us that way though we probably didn't mean it. All I could think was "It might have

---

75 Helegoland is one of a group of tiny islands in the southeastern end of the North Sea. These German islands were once possessed by Denmark and Britain. They are located about 43 miles (by sea) from the mouth of the Elbe.

been us," and from the looks of the crew something similar was going through their minds.

A pilot that lives with us was in the crowd poking around the shell of the unburning plane. He was evidently vastly excited by the spectacle and enjoying it. He called out for us to join him. Koltun answered him "you must be nuts." The same guy tried to give us details later but we all shut him up.

The wreckage lay where it had fallen for two weeks. We had to taxi by it getting set to take off for a mission and called it "our morale builder."

It had been a bad day for the group. Our tall, red-haired West Pointer operations officer, well-liked by everyone, had gone down at Hamburg along with several others.

The rumor that the group was to be broken up had been confirmed and that night we threw a farewell party that was long remembered.

It was held in the recreation hut within three blocks of where the wrecks still lay smoldering in the night.

✈

There was no time to rest, even after the horror of the previous day's crash and the poignance of the farewell party as the surviving members of the 492nd acknowledged the end of their time together. The Koltun crew was back in the air on a mission to Belgium the next day.

Here's Bud's succinct wrap up, as he writes to his folks of his time with the 492nd as the group prepared to part company:

MISSION 23
OSTEND, BELGIUM

August 7

"80% Of Our Group Has Been Shot Down"

Last mission of the 492nd group also the easiest and shortest. Carried the bombs just across the channel to Ostend which was covered with clouds and we had no radar ship. We made two circles hoping for a clear spot and came home. Got credit for the mission for which we are thankful.

Almost missed the assembly because our radio compass was out and we had no Gee box but the radio man got me a QDM (magnetic bearing to fly) and we got in formation over the North Sea.

Only three and one-half hours of flying.

80% of our group has been shot down (492nd). Just luck that we are alive.

✈

August 9, 1944

*"I'm Having A Devil of A Time Getting Myself
To Write To Anyone"*

Dear Folks,

We won't be flying for a week or so due to a big reorganization so you can leave out sweating temporarily.

Interruption—my radio operator just brought us some sandwiches from mess hall. Nice kid—he's always doing things like that.

We've had quite a bit of spare time lately and Tres has been teaching me the once terrifying mysteries of chess, a really noble game. It's a shame the time we wasted on Chinese checkers Pa, when we could have played chess. A surprising number of men here play and right now it's enjoying rather a craze.

Last night Tres and I took a longer than usual cycling expedition to a village we'd heard was the site of some unusual ruins.

On the side of a steep hill lay the village with an old Norman gateway in the center where a portcullis used to hang down in the night a thousand years ago.

On a commanding position above the village we tramped about the crumbling and in some places almost obscured remains of the Norman stronghold that had dominated this area just after the Norman conquest.[76] An informative local lad we met told us the place had been taken by storm and demolished ages ago. You could make out the line of the walls and courtyards and the citadel surrounded by a deep moat. The walls were six feet thick, of a sort of flintish stone and concrete, real cement difficult to chip. I had no idea they had building material like it in those days.

In the other end of town was another cluster of ruins, an equally old priory. The front wall of the church portion was almost intact and had the old Roman and Norman round massive arches, with little of the Gothic slenderness seen in the later cathedrals. This very large shrine must have been an impressive

---

76 The Norman Conquest of England was the invasion and then occupation of England by invading French troops (as well as an army of Norman, Breton and Flemish troops), who were led by William the Conqueror. Source: www.wikipedia.org

spot in 1086 when it was built. Now only great stumps of pillars mark its boundaries and goats nibble the lush grass on the altar while crows sit in the freely flowing air of the open windows in the one wall.

Very extensive ruins of the monk's quarters made up the rest of the site.

Some barbarians pillaged this place, or it would be in excellent shape today, the one wall shows that.

Before leaving we came back to the front gateway and stood in the doorway looking toward the main altar. Grass grew everywhere, but up the main aisle from our door to the altar a straight path had been mown. It gave the impression of soft green carpet spread before us leading us down the path to the sanctuary. The crumbling but still rugged old pillars stood against the darkening sky in which storm clouds gathered. Dusk was coming on and there was a hint of rain—we stood a while and then came back.

On the base we dropped into a neighboring hut and shared a few cookies with the lads. We mentioned our travels and a quiet fellow we didn't know very well became quite interested and gave us a very informative lecture on the places we'd seen. He also showed us notes and inscriptions he'd taken down in his bike travels in the area. He had books on architecture, one of which I'd read, and admitted to being an archeologist in training before the war. Now he's a bombardier in action.

I hadn't realized that the little churches around here were so old, but he set us straight. Almost all, at least 500-1000 years old and in excellent shape. He showed us plans to some of the cathedrals and was obviously a real student. What you won't meet up with living within 20 feet of you for the last two months!

I'm having a devil of a time getting myself to write to anyone but the family and maybe Joyce. There should be lots to tell them but the will is almost entirely absent. Combat especially is becoming a closed book except among ourselves. Anything we could tell them about it has already been told in the papers and besies, for some inexplicable reason, it seems none of their business since they are not part of it or sharing in it.

The old group has been broken up and we've been scattered all over England. I think we were disbanded because of low morale and poor bombing results. The German fighters seem to pick on our group. One theory was that since we were one of the few groups with all silver ships the fighters would gang up on us cause we were different.

They told us at the farewell gathering that the break-up was no reflection on our ability or that of our leaders—it was just "organizational" and that of course is what I wrote home.

At our new group we found out why the old 492nd had such lousy bombing—not enough training or good enough maintenance of bombing equipment.

The new group, the 445th, had bomb switches in the nose turret so the man who could see the leader the best could drop the bombs. All malfunctions of the bomb racks were investigated carefully, all crews had to go to a very interesting critique of the week's missions, and lead crews were composite crews. That is, they picked men off different crews and put them together in the lead ship after much practice together. The cream of the crop was out in front as it should have been.

They required navigators to bring back a very complete log (record of the mission) –something not stressed at all in the old group. We called it "cadet stuff" at first but found that it made us work harder and more carefully so it was for our good.

The group was old, established, with high morals, few losses and pride in its bombing record which was frequently best in the 8AAF. Its classes were very interesting and attendance was strictly enforced.

✈

Augsut 12

"One Consolation Is That Tres Was Reassigned To Our Crew"

Dear Folks,

It was with real regret we parted from the other officers we've been through so much with. Especially old Barefoot. Very often we flew beside each other and waved greetings. On the ground we always compared navigational notes and had long arguments about what route we followed when we flew above the clouds. (I learned later he was killed on his last mission.)

One consolation is that Tres was reassigned to our crew and came with us. If he hadn't come I'd be in a sad way indeed. He's quiet, inoffensive, completely unselfish, but a lot of man underneath. He's one of the few guys I've met for whom my respect has continually increased. It's been going up for six months.

Our old squadron, the 857th had the best record for bombing and least losses in the group. We were all proud of it and I liked our commander, major Heaton, a handsome, eager young West Pointer.

Just got back from some boxing exhibitions featuring Billy Conn. There was a ring rigged up in the center of a hanger and guys sat on benches or on the wings of a B-24 sitting in the hangar.

The crowd was demonstrative and enthusiastic, heartily booing half the decisions. We all had a lot of fun watching the lads get tired trying to beat each other's brains out.

MISSION 24
ZWISCHENHAHN, GERMANY

August 15

Fine day over Germany. We bombed Oldenburg airport; bombs released perfectly in train and the target area was well plastered. No flak.

Found it hard to break habits formed at the 492nd and I was advised by the squadron navigator that my log could be a lot neater and more complete.

August 17

"American Ingenuity Triumphs Again!"

Good news kids,

Koltun saw the colonel here (almost 30 years old) and told him that in our old outfit we only had to fly 30 missions. The requirement at this group is 35 but the colonel said that since we were almost done (and were from the bloody 492nd) he'd only ask 30 of us too. Really rather a wonderful break, and as a result I ought to finish in two weeks at most.

Seeing the end so close increases our nervousness somewhat of course and we're torn between wanting to get the things over quick and dreading each one more and more while looking back over the long string of lucky ones behind us.

The crew's morale has gone up to find out that they are in such a hot outfit. For a mission last week (Islands off St. Malo) the commanding general commended the group for putting 96% of the bombs on a small target in full view of our advancing ground troops.

Maybe you read Ernie Pyle's story of the air force bombing our own men on the ground preparing for the breakthrough at St. Lo. We weren't on that mission but Tres was. A terrible thing, but so easy to do when just bombing a strip of country without any big landmarks. It's impossible to see trenches or cars or anything small from 20,000.

Because they hardly ever lose any crews this group is very cramped for living quarters. Consequently four of us were shoved into a cubby hole in a Nissen hut, 15' x 7' with four iron cots and bedding but nothing except bare walls and one small window.

We stood it for six days, stumbling over our clothes and suitcases and rummaging through stacks of miscellaneous gear when we wanted a toothbrush. The pilot threw his class A blouse in a corner and we walked on it for three days before he moved it.

Then today we spent two fun-packed hours nailing six boxes (incendiary bomb crates) together to form sort of individual bureas for our clothes. We picked the boxes off a rubbish heap and used rusty nails pounded by a full-size ax to hold the weird contraptions together. With much shouting, cursing at banged fingers and general kidding we finally completed the sad deals and they now stand next our wall, efficient but rugged (must be approached with caution for the splinters and rusty nails.) American ingenuity triumphs again!

Latest rumors, confirmed by facts on every hand have us coming home quick after finishing our tour. Rest up—then for the Japs. Wonderful the way the lads are going (break through in France) unbelievable four years ago.

✈

THE LONDON UNDERGROUND

One of the things I'll always remember about England is the people of London crowded into the suffocating air of the subways to sleep while the buzz bombs were coming over.

Every night they came with their bedding and staked out a little spot; old and young, mostly poor people unnerved by the big blitz. The early ones got the double-deck bunks, the rest got the hard concrete floor and in the morning there were the old men with bare feet sleeping on the steps deep underground, sometimes without even a pillow, still in their working clothes.

The subways of London are a vast and intricate system that goes very deep down, 200 feet in some places and in all the three tube levels, on platforms and hallways you had to watch your step in the night and morning to keep from crushing a sprawled hand or foot. The trains stopped running at 12 p.m. and the air then started to foul up. By morning when we'd come by it really hit you. No ventilation when the trains stopped and the terrific humidity generated by all those deep breathing lungs, plus the smells of the great unwashed and the unabashed puddles in stray corners added up to something memorable.

Most of the Londoners decided they'd take the buzz bombs instead. Conditions are better now with the opening of the deep shelters which I have not seen.

✈

August 20

Dear Folks,

It's four o'clock on a Sunday afternoon and I'm sitting on the lower bunk craning my neck down as I write to avoid the upper.

The rain is gently falling on our tin roof and beside its pleasant patter the only sounds are the muttering of Tres and Koltun as they ponder on a game of chess.

For five days we've lived a life of ease without any missions; our time has been our own. If the orderly doesn't wake us for a mission we sleep till 10:30 or 11, usually making it to dinner. After dinner come back, lounge around a bit and then get into our shorts and play tennis or handball with GI equipment. It's the first exercise any of us have had since cadet days and has done a lot of good.

An intense, almost childish rivalry in everything we do makes every game exciting. A good example was the boxing match between pilots.

One day we were discussing boxing and immediately these two had challenged each other to a little friendly sparring. Like fools they rushed to the gym right after a big dinner and just about busted their hearts swinging at each other for half an hour with big pillow gloves. We tried to get them to take it easy but the minute one man landed a good blow they were off in a slug fest—both in full clothes, too. The pilot got a nosebleed and took the worst of it from the tall thin co-pilot.

The fight did clear the air for the two had been biting at each other a little more than usual lately.

Most of the time we four in this tiny cubby hole got along admirably despite vastly different temperaments. Koltun is big, intelligent, tough and often over-bearing but we manage to keep him insulted enough so that he's livable and his sense of humor has always come through in time to save any hard feelings from developing.

✈

August 26

Primary target (first choice) was cloud covered so we hit the second, an airport near Eindhoven in the Netherlands. Some flak but none on us. Navigated fairly well.

Navigators who aren't in the lead ship have a tougher time knowing where they are than the leaders because the lead ship flies on the gyro pilot while the followers are manually flown and hold a very erratic compass heading trying to stay in formation. The navigators try to "follow" along but with the compass often shifting 20 degrees from side to side it is difficult to know where we are going sometimes. We try to take a visual average of the readings.

I flew with Horton's crew on this mission thus getting another one ahead of my old crew.

We came home alone through the thick haze when the nose gunner got a stomach cramp.

Pilot asked me if it was o.k. to come home alone and I said "sure." The trouble was that the next minute the nose gunner decided he was too sick to stay in his turret and he climbed out scattering all my maps and data sheets in the big wind when he opened the turret door. We were over the North Sea at the time and close to England but I got straightened out in time to come in with the aid of the Gee box.

✈

August 27

Dear Folks,

What a crew we've got. A month ago I found some gray hairs in my co-pilot's curly locks and today he pulled a silver one from among my thinning fuzz.

The pilot—though not yet 22 has terribly thin top cover and his scaly dome can be seen easily from any angle. We all may be sent home to help with the billiard ball shortage.

Say folks, the last time I was in London I managed to take in the bloody old tower of London. What a grim history it has.

We were taken in hand (about 100 Americans) by one of the Beef-eaters in his traditional costume.

The "Tower of London" is actually a group of towers and barracks surrounded by a wall and remnants of a moat.

The principal building was finished in 1076 by William the Conqueror and is in excellent shape. This main building is called the "White Tower" and is the one they always show on the postcards as being the "Tower of London."

It is now filled with a few suits of armor and ancient weapons, but is otherwise quite bare. We weren't shown any crown jewels. In fact, the tour gave us very few views of the interior of the buildings. We were merely privileged to hear that "in the room behind that window in that wall Sir Joe Doakes was stabbed while at his prayers—here is the spot where Ann Boleyn, wife of Henry the VIII was beheaded in the private execution accorded only to the nobility—common men were killed outside the wall in public view.

We've made our ascetics cell a lot more livable lately with pictures of the family hanging and a fair share of the clothes on our hooks.

One of our rehabilitation projects didn't work too well however. We got a broom stick and placed it with one end on one double decker bunk and one end on the other. Then we tied it down and hung our clothes hangers on it. It was soon covered with weighted hangers and had a graceful swaybacked effect.

Came the night and sweet dreams from which we were all yanked awake by a heavy "Bang!" and a following crash. Rapid-fire conjectures filled the darkness—someone suggested we'd been run into by a jeep at least. No one got up to find out.

Morning revealed the shattered broomstick and our clothes on the floor. Too much had been too much.

We're so cramped for space and are so extremely garrulous (each knows the other's most intimate secrets now) that the atmosphere is hardly conducive to letter writing.

✈

Have been making myself less loved lately by waking up the lads when I catch them asleep in the afternoon by shouting "flak, flak" in their ear and watching them jump.

✈

Ah yes, Tres, our erstwhile bombardier, being much on the ball, has been put on a lead crew just as at our last base serving as nose turret gunner and assistant as he's already behind and lead crews only fly about one out of every three missions.

Really didn't leave this till the end purposely but I've been promoted to first Lt. which is a nice comfortable sort of rank, no? It means a pay increase of $25.00 (six pounds and ten shillings.) Jean no longer outranks me.

✈

Often we sit around together discussing the old 492nd and wonder why it is we are still alive.

The very first day at that group they told us to show up at a certain building the next morning for an orientation lecture.

Koltun and everybody else overslept the next morning and we were half an hour late for the lecture. The officer that was to speak gave us a highly deserved bawling out that none of us forgot because he said, "I've noticed that crews that get off to a bad start here by being late for appointments are the ones that screw up and get shot down." We naturally resented a morale building speech like that, especially on our second day at a combat group, but we are here today and God only knows where that officer is for he was shot down months ago.

MISSION 25
GRANIENBURG, GERMANY

August 27

"Have Begun to Feel Like Part of The Team Here"

Mission was briefed for Berlin and I was all set with a brand new flak-chart I had worked on all afternoon the day before. It gave the locations and amount of flak for all of Europe within range.

The whole 8th AAF was on the way but had to turn back at the Danish coast because of insurmountable clouds.

We poked around the shoreline a while looking for a hole and caught a little flak off the Isle of Sylt.

I worked hard and followed the lead fairly well even making a good log. Have begun to feel like part of the team here and rejoice in the excellence of the outfit.

After landing I walked around the plane as usual to see if we had any holes and discovered one in my compartment. A mechanic was standing next to me as I pointed it out to the crew. He said "Now I know why I was so glad when I washed out of the cadets."

Two missions to go and very grateful to be alive and unhurt, but somewhat depressed by future prospects and the swiftly coming day when wars will cease and I will say "Now what?"

ABORTION ON SEPTEMBER 1

Got 80 miles inside Allied occupied France and had to turn back because of weather. Nice to fly over most of France now without the tension you get when over enemy territory.

September 1

"Hang In There, And The End Is In Sight."

Dear Folks,

Another autumn is here and our skies are filled with the tumbling cumulus billows that we scarcely saw all summer. The showers are more sudden and severe and there is constantly a damp chill in the air despite an unusual bit of sunshine.

I'm still being impressed by the excellence of this group. Pa, I remember you telling me once that organization was the key to success in any enterprise and boy this is an example.

Some former commander at this base set up elaborate conditioning schools and training programs for new crews and the forms he built up have continued and been improved on, with a result that this group's lead crews are tops and no one is sent out till he's been thoroughly checked.

At our old outfit everything was very haphazard, and it was obvious to us all that the best crews were not leading, but things just went on, crews came and went, and nothing was done. It is to the 8th AAF's credit that they broke up the organization.

The two groups have been a very forceful example to us of what a little planning and leadership can do.

We hadn't been to the beach-head area for a long time but recently we went in that way and got a good look. It was nice to be able to fly by Caen without being shot at anymore.

The location of the recent entrapment of the Nazis 7th army (Falaise trap[77]) looks as peaceful as ever with a few exceptions. Once in a while the green fields and orchards will encompass a small area, dust colored amidst the green, that is completely pot-marked as though the earth had a spotty kind of small-pox.

One spot was so covered with craters of all sizes that nothing was left growing. We flew by many villages. Most seemed untouched but occasionally one drifted by with the familiar white blank areas among the houses—blank except for the ugly rubble of broken walls still standing.

Hang in there, and the end is in sight.

✈

"The Robot Bomb Menace to London Has Almost Gone"

Well Folks,

If it had not been for that last change in stations, we should all be finished now and coming home, but because of the delay it

---

77 The "Falaise Trap" refers to the Battle of the Falaise Pocket, (in the Falaise, Calvados area in Normandy, France) in which Nazi troops were surrounded by the Western Allies in a deadly and decisive battle that helped open up the area leading to occupied Paris. Source: wikipedia.org/FalaisePocket

entailed we are now entering the period of rotten flying weather with these few last missions still hanging fire.

We've had a foretaste of what winter in England is like and it's not for us.

We're all getting cabin fever in this cramped room, sitting hour after hour trying to amuse ourselves. A game of chess and then a game of gin rummy and if the weather is good a game of tennis or handball. I read a bit of Plato and have managed to keep from banging my head on the wall but I wish to hell we'd finish those last few or hear of the Nazis' collapse.

It's really a fantastically soft life and if I were ambitious I could put in real study in our hours of free time, but there is so little to do and so much to do it in that the slightest task is postponed and I've been three weeks thinking about fixing my bike tire though the weather has been so bad I couldn't have gone anywhere.

As a result of no bike I've had to take our laundry on foot to a helpful farm woman I discovered. The army service is two weeks so I have this woman help out. Her time is one day.

She told us the civilian soap ration was very small so we bring her all our extra plus paying plenty for her work.

The road to this farm leads through a village that has the usual ancient Norman church. This one is quite distinctive, however, as the church tower (to which the building was added in later times) is a 1000 years old, round in shape and a former Saxon lookout tower, now crumbling but still holding its bells.

A bit curious about the interior I came up through the yard and swung open the heavy creaking oak door that led me into the subdued light and reverent quiet of the inside. Most of the pews were almost worn through from the squirmings of generations that had occupied them.

In the east to catch the light of Sunday morning's sun was the one stained glass window in the place: a remarkably good job for such a spot it seemed to us.

Beneath the window an altar, rightly clothed in silk, spread across the window's portion of the room. A large gold cross stood on the table.

I tiptoed around though no one else was about and got an awful start when the door swung shut with the wind.

I've been encouraging in myself a feeling of gratefulness to the powers that be that I'm still intact. It's partly the result of a superstitious fear that if I don't seem thankful the fates may no longer smile upon me, but anyway I'm grateful and I never felt it any more than I did alone in that little church.

The robot bomb menace to London has almost gone, so we can take our next leave there without feeling a little guilty for needlessly exposing ourselves and causing trouble.

Finally, the long break in England ended, and the missions started up again. Here's Bud's take on the mission to Karlsruhe, as the crew re-entered the action and the letters home resume.

MISSION 26
KARLSRUHE, GERMANY

September 8

"We Got a Good Look At Paris From 12,000 Feet"

Dumped five 1000 pounders perfectly on RR yards at Karlsruhe Germany in the Seigfried line. After dodging through clouds all the way the target was open and we had a nice run. Little flak but none on us. Many ships had trouble with their bombs. Temperature was -40 degrees when we had to climb to 26,000 feet to get through a cloud deck.

Coming back, we got a good look at Paris from 12,000 feet, once again in French hands. I saw the Eiffel Tower and the crew saw the Champs Elysees with the Arch de Triomphe.

After Karlsruhe the boys had a brief break and then were headed back to Germany on a mission to Ulm.

Bud's run of 30 missions was accomplished on September 30, 1944. Here, with an ironic hint of poignance, he offers his thoughts on the events of his last mission. At age 22, Bud was soon to become an army veteran. The months of active duty served by the Koltun crew were likely the most dramatic of these young men's lives, and they all knew they were lucky to be alive.

MISSION 27
ULM, GERMANY

September 10

"Dagood Brought Her in For The Last Time"

Last mission for me though the crew has two more to go. I felt so good I didn't wear a flak suit till we were in the target area—foolish tempting of fate.

Target was cloud covered and we bombed by radar but all the way in across France it was clear so I had a fine time watching the scenery go by and letting the towns show up on my ETAs (estimated time of arrival).

At this time the battle line was near Metz and Verdun, marked by flak as we came across.

A mile ahead of us near Verdun we watched a B-24 turn into a dirty blob of oily flame and smoke that drifted shapelessly down the four miles of air to the ground. No one got out.

Passing Verdun[78] ourselves we all exchanged excited comments at the sight of the old trench systems from the first war still visible in the forests.

On the way home we passed by Stuttgart which suddenly began to jump and mushroom into black smoke as a slew of delayed action bombs went off before us.

I sang for the crew from France home though they didn't seem too enthused about it as they aren't done.

Dagood brought her in for the last time with me aboard.

---

78 Bud's mention of the old trench systems refers to those created during World War I for the bloody Battle of Verdun, which was waged from February 21 to December 18, 1916.

The crew cordially invited me to fly with them on their last missions but I refused the invitation with enthusiasm and immediately went to London for a few days.

All the crew survived their tour of operations with the 8th AAF though Tressler didn't finish up for several months.

I learned later that the luck of the 445th finally ran out and in October they lost 20 out of 30 planes on one mission when the Germans came up in force to offer battle for just about the last time.

Our wounded gunner had his flak riddled finger fixed up and finished up in Italy. His replacement, Green, who flew on every mission with us after the 14th, came through in good condition.

In two weeks I was home in Bismarck on leave as I was fortunate being returned by plane, rather than the longer trip on shipboard.

By October 1944, Bud's active duty as a navigator and bombardier flying missions over Europe was over. The Koltun crew had survived the war, and the men would spend the rest of their days wondering why they had been the ones who made it. Bud survived the war physically unscathed, but would forever, with quiet stoicism, mourn the death of the many men with whom he had served.

CHAPTER 4

Bud's Adventure with the Air Transport Command

*A*fter September 30, there is a long break between the letters and diary entries, as Bud was released from active duty once the crew's 30 mission assignment was fulfilled.

Bud was offered a chance to continue his service in Japan, as the conflict there continued to rage until V-J Day ("Victory over Japan") but he declined the offer. Without a doubt, he'd had enough bombing missions to last for the rest of his life.

Another offer did intrigue him, however. The 8AAF offered Bud the job of working with the Air Transport Command (ATC), as part of a crew delivering supplies to military stations throughout Europe and the Middle East.

The ATC was the worldwide air transport system created after the 1941 attack on Pearl Harbor, when the US was suddenly thrust into two major wars. The ATC, which was developed with help from the major airlines and aircraft manufacturers, was responsible for bringing equipment, supplies and personnel to key allied military stations overseas.

The ATC was a massive operation. By the time of Bud's involvement in the ATC in 1945, the command involved over 209,000 military personnel as well as 104,000 civilians. Bud was assigned to the ATC's oldest route, which involved the Northern Africa and Middle Eastern theaters of the war.

BUD'S ADVENTURE WITH THE AIR TRANSPORT COMMAND

Bud takes off with the Air Transport Command, headed for the North African and Middle Eastern theaters. (The "Hot Rock" referred to a cartoon strip Bud saved, about the navigator's role in bombing missions.

LETTERS FROM BUD

Bud's work with the ATC began in the spring of 1945. Freed from the stress and emotional conflicts of serving on bombing missions, Bud was now able to more thoroughly enjoy the adventure of traveling the world. His buoyant spirit shines through in his letters home during his travels across the globe with the ATC, as the war finally wound down to its ultimate conclusion.

The first part of Bud's service involved a run through the Pacific, touching down with deliveries at military sites that had been ravaged by the war. In this section Bud describes a visit to the tiny island of Tarawa, which had been the site of a terrible battle between Allied forces and alarmingly well-prepared Japanese forces. In this record of his travels, he also visits the graves of young men from back home, killed in battle and buried in Hawaii. Now age 23, there's no doubt Bud and the men he served with had already seen and survived more than their share of the harsh realities of war, and of life itself.

Map showing an itinerary for an upcoming ATC trip, along with Bud's official navigation license.

BUD'S LETTERS HOME FOLLOWING
TWO ATC DELIVERY FLIGHTS
JUNE, JULY AND AUGUST 1945

"The Pilot Was a Charming Fellow"

June 23, 1945

Dear folks,

This afternoon at three we finally arrived at Memphis again after 60 hours of almost continuous flying from the South Pacific where we delivered a C-46 (huge twin engined Curtiss Wright transport.)

The whole trip was quite uneventful but interesting and often fun, thanks to a fine crew.

The pilot was a charming fellow about 35 who had 600 hours flying the same type ship over the "hump"[79] in India-Burma-China and was covered with medals. At first he seemed merely charming but he had a stiff spine underneath and was an expert pilot. He had seldom flown with a navigator and was an old hand, but he took my heading and held them till I told him to change. I worked hard for him and had the satisfaction of his appreciation.

---

79 The "hump" was an extremely dangerous route flown by the ATC as they took supplies to US Army Air Forces stationed in China (as well as to military units that were part of the Chinese war effort of Chiang Kai-shek.) This route took ATC planes over the eastern end of the Himalayas, with limited information for navigation and without reliable geographic charts or information on weather. Pilots with a successful record of flying over "the hump" would surely have been seen as living legends in WW 2 air force circles. Source: https://en.wikipedia.org/wiki/The_Hump

An Egyptian leather case Bud haggled over in Cairo. After the war he gave the case to his mother, and then later passed it on to his daughter, Molly, with a hand-written note commenting on his war experiences.

We also had a Sgt. Radio operator and a Sgt. Engineer. The engineer went to sleep as soon as we took off and slept during most of the jumps until we landed. The radio man was the most hard-working of us all as he had to continually be sending in position reports and weather given by me.

We flew together on an American Airliner to Salinas, California, where we got our skip and took off on the scenic route down the California Coast from Monterey to Los Angeles.

One thing after another went wrong with the plane at the field in Long Beach and day after day we lounged on the beach in the afternoon.

Bud and one of his pals yukking it up at a party in Long Beach while on leave.

One morning was taken by me in alignment of the navigation instruments[80] on the ship with its longitudinal axis. The simple little semi-periscope and grid lines with which we watch the ground go by and tell how many degrees the wind is blowing us off course, has to be in line with the plane. The same is true for the device by which we tell which way the plane is going by taking bearings on the sun. By it we check the accuracy of our magnetic compasses.

The plane was finally ready to go but we wanted to make a trial fuel consumption flight so one day we took the beautiful route up the Owens Valley north to Reno and back. This valley lies just to the east of the Sierra Nevada mountain range which includes among its peaks Mt. Whitney, the highest in America. Just out of sight on the right was Death Valley, 200 feet below sea level.

All of us took turns flying the ship and a cumbersome brute it was. Without a gyro pilot ("George") on a long flight it would have been a man killer.

The pilot got quite excited as we twisted our way along with these great snow-capped ranges towering a mile above us on Death Valley. In fact, he turned out to be quite a soldier of fortune though from his good English I would never have thought so.

Flying up mountain valleys you do not get nearly the impression of grandeur and power from the peaks as you do standing on the ground. Perhaps it's because the relative height is so much less—also because the mighty piles of rock from the dune just drift by you like anything else.

---

80 Bud's notes on navigation and the precision of the instruments he used to plot the plane's route show the skill and level of responsibility required of the navigators in the pre-computer World War II era.

High point of the trip was flying over Lake Tahoe. The pilot showed us Emerald Bay and the fabulous lodges tucked away in the tree-lined coves. The water was a pure dark blue with scarcely a ripple on it, giving back a perfect reflection of the forested hills on shore.

A thing most navigators have to worry about is getting their pilot's confidence, so he'll take the orders given without any arguments. Some navigators aren't any good and some pilots, all of whom get a lot of navigation in their training, think they can do better going it alone or depending on the radio if there is one in the area.

Well, we came to a little town on the floor of the valley and the pilot says it is Bishop and goes down to look at a hotel he used to stay in. After circling the town a bit he says it isn't Bishop because he can't see the hotel. We'd been flying up and down valleys and around peaks and I'd been just watching a map occasionally – but I couldn't miss with all those mountains to go by. I decided this was a time to get a plug in for myself so I made sure I knew which town it was from all the features and the time we'd been flying that direction and then I told him he was right the first time, it was Bishop. He didn't believe it and neither did the co-pilot so I told them to go on and try to find the town over the next range. They didn't find it – admitted they were wrong and didn't give any more trouble. (Somebody's got to beat my drum here).

The next night we all assembled and were briefed, given weather maps, etc., all the navigators were busy figuring long after the rest of the crew went to the plane. From the winds they gave us, we figured how much to correct for its effect, how long it would take us to make Oahu—how much gas it would take—and at what point in the route it would be better to go on instead of back in case of trouble.

The sun had just set when the pilot dragged all that gas and airplane off the field and into a fine clear night.

About every one and one-half hours I'd rouse myself from a semi-dose with my head on the desk and get up in the plastic dome to shoot the stars. Then down to the table and columns of figures and there we are where the lines cross in a fix, right on course. Then a position report for the radio man plus the weather (wind direction from the celestial position, clouds, temperature)—eat an orange, tell the pilot we're doing o.k. and back to the desk.

The eastern stars rose and the western stars fell. Once the great showy band of the Milky Way stood directly overhead. I used Jupiter and Polaris and Alpheratz and Fomalhaut and Venus[81], the morning star, just as the dawn was breaking. Half way over the wind shifted radically from the forecast and I corrected him twice—the only times in 14 hours of flying.

Came the dawn. Because of little dust or haze at our altitude the line of the sunlit sky and the darkness was almost as definite as when a black curtain is slowly raised on a bright stage. Complete darkness with the stars pricking through and then the next time I looked a strip of white and yellow behind us with the blackness above. I had little time for looking as it is essential to get a good fix before daylight, to come in on.

All we did was sleep in Oahu, though before I did that I discovered an old cadet classmate—honor man of our class who

---

81 Bud's fascination with and keen knowledge of astronomy was a huge asset in his work as a navigator. It remained a lifelong passion for him, as he continued studying the stars (with the help of a sophisticated Celestron telescope) for the rest of his life.

rode with Gannon and me from Colorado to Mass. We recounted adventures and saw a lot of each other on the next legs.

The remaining hops were in daylight with only the sun, driftmeter and stop watch (get our speed) to keep us on course — plus the faithful radio compass, of course, when we got close to destination.

Goal for the first day was Christmas Island, a forlorn little coral reef south of Hawaii. The island was covered with palms and riding on a truck to go swimming saw all sorts of broad-leaved plants and bushes and land crabs that went scurrying awkwardly along. The swim in the warm water of the lagoon was excellent.

At night we sat in the open air theater and gazed at the strange new stars in the sky before the show started. The Southern Cross and Rigial Kentaurus[82] were high in the sky and very bright.

On the way to Canton Island the next day we were initiated into that not very select crowd who have crossed the equator[83]. I walked into the cockpit and told the pilots we would cross the equator in about 10 minutes, then I went back to the desk. A moment later I turned around to see the pilot behind me with a cup full of pink fluid that I mistook for nectar. Actually it was hydraulic fluid which he calmly poured down my neck while I just calmly sat there.

---

82 Here Bud refers to Rigel Kentaurus (better known as Alpha Centauri, which is the third brightest star (actually a star system) in the sky and the closest star system to earth. Source: www.space.com

83 Historically, members of the navy who crossed the equator during their service were put through an initiation ceremony, often in the presence of a person dressed in the role of King Neptune. This is a reference to the rituals practiced in ancient times, when mariners would offer animal sacrifices to appease the King of the sea, lest those sailors who passed Northwest Africa (the deep unknown) fall off the sharp edge of the known world. By World War II, the ceremony was a playful ritual that still acknowledged a true rite of passage, which is why Bud refers to it here in a joking fashion. Source: www.ww2db.com

BUD'S ADVENTURE WITH THE AIR TRANSPORT COMMAND

Canton Island was the end of the universe. A ten-mile lagoon surrounded by a coral strip just wide enough to put a runway on. There was one tree on the island—a cocoanut palm which the old classmate and I climbed at sunset after a stroll on the beach. For the first time I saw what made sea shells that way. We walked down that beach and everywhere saw sea shells rolling and walking along. The critter inside is very mean looking and has claws, sort of like a crab.

From the look-out platform on the palm we could look over the whole island and the calm but cruelly limitless sea stretching away in all directions to the perfect line of the horizon. Vast billowing thunderheads were scattered over the sky and as the sun set we watched the orange glow travel to their very tops and then disappear.

The next day my hard work navigating paid off since the radio beacon that helps guide us in went off the air and we came in on dead-reckoning and the sun. That white line of surf (the only thing to look for coming into these flat islands) sure looked good.

The place was Tarawa, site of our flookiest battle[84] on the basis of men killed per hour. 1,500[85] in a three-day fight on an island three miles long and 800 yards wide at its widest.

Arriving early in the afternoon we ate and donned our shorts and GI shoes for a reconnaissance mission on foot. I was much interested since in Texas I read the book on the battle here and

---

84 The Battle of Tarawa took place on two days in November of 1943. It is estimated that 6,400 American, Japanese and Korean lives were lost in this fight on the tiny island of Betio, located in the southwest area of the Tarawa Atoll. The battle was said to be the first time the American military encountered serious pushback from the Japanese during the Pacific War. The Americans staged an amphibious landing on the island but were met by a well prepared Japanese military force. The harrowing battle saw heavy casualties for the US Military, as Bud and his friends discovered on their visit to the island. Source: https://en.wikipedia.org/wiki/Battle_of_Tarawa
85

had a rough idea where things happened. Right behind our hut was the murderous beach where the first wave of marines waded ashore into the muzzles of the machine guns. They had to wade because the water that day was too low for most of the landing boats to pass over the reef. The shallow water just off shore was still littered with wrecked tanks and landing boats red with rust, their steel sides punctured like cardboard by shells of all sizes.

It had been such a pleasant trip so far that no one felt very solemn and we horsed around while reading the signs explaining points of heavy losses and the tactical situation. I was naturally giving a running lecture to supplement the signs.

Most of the Jap pill-boxes[86] had been torn down to make room for the runway which almost covers the whole island, but a few were left on the beach and we nosed about them all, noting the strong construction.

Further on down the beach we came to the first white crosses with which the rest of the island is covered. There were about 20 in the first little patch in neatly tended rows. The first name I saw set me back on my heels. Right in the front row in cold, black type on that white cross it said William E. Brandenburg, Pvt. He was in the second marines and died on the first day's fighting November 20, 1943.

On the west end as we rounded the isle to come back the other way we examined great 6 and 8 inch coast defense guns from Singapore the Japs had installed. To little avail however, as a battle ship at 12,000 yards range put them all out of action with the second salvo.

---

86 Pill boxes were prepared, dug-in guard posts made of concrete. The structures had "loopholes" for use in firing weapons at enemy forces. These structures provided protection for soldiers as they fired from a trench position.
Source: en.wikipedia.org/wiki/Pillbox_(military)

At this end all the pillboxes and wastage from the battle had been piled. What a junkyard it was; ruined guns, ruined fortresses, ruined machines and ruined men or parts of them. Just a few bones in with the broken helmets and empty shell cases, one thigh bone and numerous ribs. Friends or enemies, who can say?

All the way around the island we had noticed little windmills made of wood set up to do the men's laundry. Their one-foot blades spun merrily in the sea breeze moving a plunger up and down in a barrel full of clothes by means of an eccentric.

We swam and slept and left that dearly purchased strip of coral. The pilot let me take off the next morning (runway is 200 yards wide) and I got a big kick out of it.

All morning we flew dodging thunderstorms and then came into green, steaming, mist-covered Quadalcanal.

Everyone else was tired from yesterday's jaunt so by myself I hitch-hiked on jeeps and trucks and finally worked down to the cemetery a couple of hundred yards from the beach where the guys from the 184th are buried with their marine comrades.

They really have done justice by the lads. The clearing consists of about 10 acres surrounded by tall and stately palms and covered with a well-tended lawn. In the center of the armies of crosses is a chapel made of thatched palm leaves. A white fence surrounds the area.

Bushy haired natives were pushing lawn mowers about when I entered and started to look for our regiment. The crosses seemed to form an endless avenue and I wandered aimlessly looking.

Just as I was about to give up, I found Lew Hamery, Dick Smith and John Weigel, all in the same corner and close together.

Their folks need have no fears that their graves are neglected. It was a beautiful spot—between the mountains and the sea.

In the morning we took off for New Guinea, passed Fulagi and over the famous "slot" where the Tokyo Express[87] used to run. The last we saw of Quadalcanal[88] was Cape Esperance—the grass on its hills still pock-marked by hundreds of shell craters, so thick they overlap. The scars of this war take a long time to heal even in jungle country.

By the time we got to destination two days later we were getting used to the calls in the jungle at night. The heat wasn't too bad as it is winter down there now and insects didn't bother us much though we always slept under netting.

Our destination was an island off New Guinea (Biak). We stayed just one day but by the use of a jeep we saw quite a bit of it.

We started on this jaunt about sunset and rode for miles by all sorts of installations—little villages of engineers along the road, navy harbor men and flak batteries, etc... Further on out of the populated district we rode along the assault beaches where more Americans had died taking another base; another step.

The moon was up, quite pale in an overcast sky and a pyramid of searchlights followed a tiny silver plane along as we came back. Both the road and beach were lined by ghoulish looking dead trees, killed by shell fire. They were white and leafless, thrusting shattered bony fingers in every direction.

---

87 The Tokyo Express refers to the ships of the Imperial Japanese navy, which were used for night deliveries of military supplies to Japanese forces in New Guinea and the Solomon Islands as the Pacific campaign of World War II was waged. Source: wikipedia.org

88 The Battle of Guadalcanal (codenamed "Operation Watchtower") was the first major military offensive brought by the Allies against Japan. The battle was waged between August 7, 1942 and February of 1943. Source: Wikipedia.org

The next morning, we took a jeep again to look over this beach in daylight.

Down on the shore on the edge of the jungle even early in the morning the humidity was almost unbearable. We no more than set foot on shore than the whole beach seemed to crawl. All sorts of tiny creeping things began to squirm away underfoot. One lizard jumped around on the water like a kangaroo on land, so fast it was hard to follow.

The beach was fairly clean with only a few rusting cartridges and an occasional bone about. Those first nights in the jungle our men must have needed healthy nerves.

We came back the 3000 miles in 40 hours of almost continuous flying. Right in over the Golden Gate.

From the South Pacific and then back to California, Bud's time with the ATC run was thrilling, fascinating, heart-breaking and utterly sobering. Yet there was still much more to come, as after a short break, he was off again, this time for lands unknown, in the mysterious Middle East.

In India, Morocco and Egypt, Bud played the role of a stranger in a strange land; a Yankee innocent wandering the dusty Middle Eastern street bazaars and finding friendship and adventure on every corner. Bud's innate curiosity and his "common touch" — his ability to relate as an equal to anyone he ever met — served him well in his travels at the end of the war, and for the rest of his life.

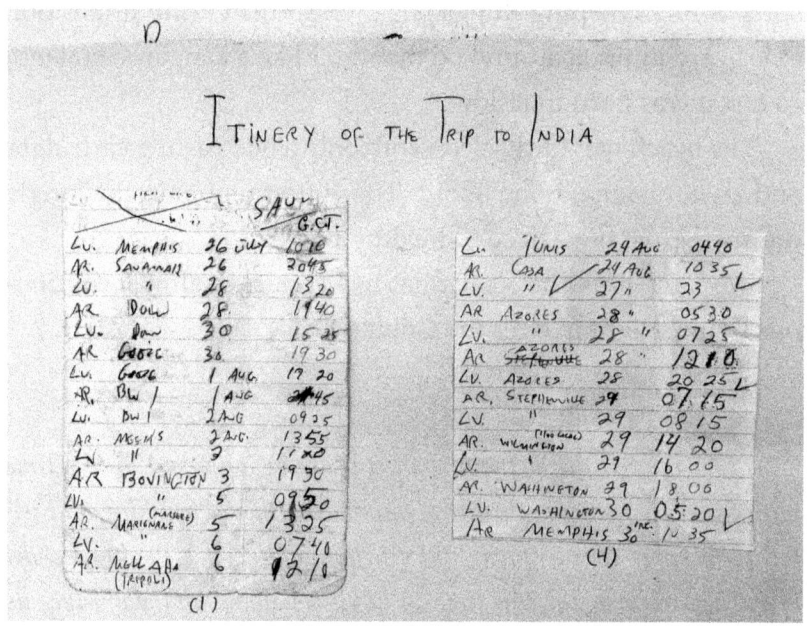

One of Bud's hand-scrawled flight itineraries, this one for the upcoming trip to India.

RETURN

"Yes Sahib and no Sahib."

Two days later the plane was delivered, the crew had been sent upon its way, and I was dead-heading back (riding as passenger).

Two things we won't forget about India are the "yes Sahib and no Sahib." Always Sahib, which means "Master."

The other item was the oriental practice of always telling you what you want to hear, whether it is true or not. I was fouled up many times by asking a native if I was on the right road. They always said yes. According to the guide book, it is considered impolite to give an answer that would be unpleasant to me.

CASABLANCA

"We Had a Merry Time"

We spent 3 days in this Atlantic port waiting for the "green" project of infantry men to be flown home so they could put us on.

We took a tour of the native quarter including the Sultan's magnificent gardens where Roosevelt and Churchill[89] got together.

Most exciting item on the tour was an exclusive visit to the Medina, off-limits to common folk, but seen by us because we ran into some full colonels who had heard about it.

---

[89] US President Franklin Delano Roosevelt and UK Prime Minister Winston Churchill met in 1943 (from January 14 to 24) at the Anfa Hotel in Casablanca (in French Morocco) for what was called the "Casablanca Conference." The purpose of the conference was to discuss the Allied strategy for the ongoing war in Europe. Source: www.Wikipedia.com/Casablance_Conference.

The colonels talked the MP's into a visit without any trouble and we had a merry time.

The Medina[90] was a white-washed, spotless, walled enclosure in which the French authorities confined the women they picked off the streets for not having the proper papers.

They were of all races and color with French, Jew and Arab predominating. They had one thing in common, a complete absence of any false modesty.

The grey-headed, paunchy old colonels hardly bargained for the time they got. The girls seized upon them as the richest and the brass had a hard time preserving its dignity as swarms of impish women closed in on them with cat-calls and pokes and cries for cigarettes.

BACK TO U.S.

"Just Couldn't Charge The Guy $50"

Aside from losing an engine on a flight from the Azores and having to turn back, our Atlantic crossing was uneventful. In the Azores[91] I bought a Swiss watch for 26 dollars and sold it in Memphis for $49.95 (just couldn't charge the guy $50.)

---

90 Many cities in North Africa would have a walled-off area called a "Medina Quarter." These areas had narrow, maze-like streets that were too narrow for cars or even motorcycles. Originally these areas would have been used to keep out invaders. In the area Bud observed, the authorities used the walled off area to try to keep street women captive, with interesting and apparently unexpected results. https://en.wikipedia.org/wiki/Medina_quarter

91 The Azores are a storied set of Islands deep in the Atlantic ocean that inspired many myths and tall tales of Utopia, since "the early days of classical antiquity." Source: https://en.wikipedia.org/wiki/History_of_the_Azores

MEMPHIS

"Washington... A Kind of Tired Air About The Place"

30 Aug 45

Back at last. Just came in an hour ago after a 5-hour flight from Washington where I spent the afternoon walking my legs off. I saw the Washington monument, white dull brick buildings and a kind of tired air about the place.

"They Had a Much Nicer Camp Than We"

From Bangor we headed north up over the St. Lawrence, across the lake-spotted greenery of Labrador to Goose Bay on the Hamilton river.

Compared to the really oppressive heat and humidity of Memphis, Goose Bay was delightful. The crisp air and pine trees standing at the very edge of camp helped emphasize the sense of peaceful isolation you couldn't miss because all the way from the St. Lawrence there is nothing.

We met a matronly Wac Lt. who invited us to visit the Canadian camp on an inspection of their hobby shop. The pilot and I tagged along and spent a delightful evening poking around their establishment. They had a much nicer camp than we.

At the Officer's Club we had freshly caught salmon fried in flour—delicious.

We rode back to our camp in a jeep over rough roads and watched the northern lights flap around.

One nice thing about the sub-arctic is the long duration of twilight and sunset. The light fades imperceptibly over the pines and lakes until you see only the silhouettes of trees.

GREENLAND

"They Were a Perfect Whiteness Against The Dark Sea"

We flew to Greenland in broad daylight over the usual solid undercast until 20 miles off the coast when it began to break-up and we could see the water flecked with icebergs.

Coming in to our field (Bluie West 1[92]) was quite an adventure involving a 50-mile flight up a twisting fiord and a final landing at a field which was crowded unto the space between the end of the fiord—a great glacier—and some mountains.

The trip up that fiord offered some noble sights. The water became more crowded with icebergs—the farthest we went between the mountains. We saw one that was easily a mile long and 1/3 of a mile wide. They were a perfect whiteness against the dark sea.

We finally rounded the last bend in the fiord and there lay the field; just as the briefing movie in Goode-bay had shown it.

The pilot got a kick out of the runway, it was at sea level on one end and 160 feet high on the other due to the slant of the shore.

What a place that was—The fiord in front—the glacier behind and mountains on both sides. From the top of one of them

---

92 The US military airfield in Greenland was given the codename "Bluie," in the 1930s when the US navy gave special names (in alphabetical order) to areas of significance for the armed forces. The name "Bluie" (with the direction and number of the base following the name) was used by military radiomen to identify landing sites. The codename was easier to pronounce than the actual old Norse or Inuit names of the areas. Source: https://en.wikipedia.org/wiki/Bluie .

a good-sized waterfall tumbled. I have no idea what furnished the water.

With no regret we left that chilly, damp desolation the next morning. The soldiers who sit in deserted spots like that all over the world deserve a lot of credit.

The fiord was three miles wide with mountains on all sides going up to 1500 feet and beyond. Low clouds hung at 1000 feet covering the mountain tops. These dirty patches of scud blew in while we were getting out to the plane. We took the runway and across the ice-filled water, making a slow climbing turn so we could rundown the fiord and get enough altitude to cross the mountains hemming us in. We poked our nose into the clouds "sniffing them out" but they were thick, so we came down again.

All of us had tensed up a bit and everyone was now huddled around the pilot telling him where mountains were; me with a crumpled map in hand pointing out directions. The pilot finally got a bright idea and getting over near the left side of the fiord he put the plane into a fast dive and then pulled up in a steep climbing turn to the right, an actual chandelle[93]. This put us over the middle of the fiord lumbering up through the grey blanket. Instantly we were in a solid nothingness and the pilot was on instruments.

The anxious moments were few tho, for we quickly broke into the golden sunlight and saw we would have missed the mountain we were afraid of even if we hadn't come through the cloud so fast. The sun felt good in any event.

East we go again, across the tip of Greenland's mighty ice-cap. The coastline is guarded by a border range of mountains

---

93 The Chandelle maneuver was an 180 degree "climbing" turn. It was originally developed by pilots in France during World War I. The maneuver aids in a quick escape after the release of bombs on enemy territory. Source: http://simfliteminnesota.blogspot.com/2007/01/teaching-chandelle-it-works-in-sim-too.html

cut by fiords. Inside this cup lie the snow fields of the icecap, a vast plain of whiteness whose own weight upon itself pushes the wrinkled, graceful curves of glaciers down the fiords. Here great pieces drop off to form our icebergs. I watched carefully the end of the glacier but didn't see any pieces actually drop.

It was about time for some K-rations[94] anyway. We lunched continually on the whole trip. They put about 10 cartons aboard and I'm very fond of them[95].

Iceland was still the bleak, rock, flatland under the same dull-gray sky as last year.

ENGLAND

"You Can't Beat The English"

Boy, did England look good! We gassed up in Scotland and then landed for the night just outside London, a very nice break.

We came in just a bit after sunset and parked in the grass off the concrete. When the engines finally stopped and we stepped out into that balmy air I felt like singing, tired as I was.

It was completely still and in the quiet we looked around at the woods bordering the field. The wooded parks and small neat fields, a misty blue in the distance, surrounded us once more.

---

94 K-Rations were prepackaged, non-perishable cartons of food (one ration provided for breakfast, lunch and dinner) developed as an easy to carry food ration for soldiers. Bud's oddball fondness for these prepackaged meals continued for the rest of his life, as he was known to stock up on canned rations (including canned fruitcake) sold in Army surplus stores years after the war, in an attempt to convince his skeptical children of the products' usefulness as a cheap food source. Source: http://www.kration.info

95

There was no room on the base so we drew billets[96] in town at famed Grosvenor Square. By the time we had eaten at my old officer's club off Piccadilly it was 11 p.m. but my pilot wanted to sightsee. We walked to Trafalgar Square under the brilliant glare of a street lighting system that would take a back seat to no one's. Despite our exhaustion we were all quite excited and I recall exclaiming always at the amount of light and comparing it to the old days of blackout[97].

Of course I had to show the lads Piccadilly[98]. The traffic pattern there of street-walkers and soldiers is always a thing of amused fascination to Americans. There is so much haggling over prices and buying and selling of bodies I used to think of it as a modern slave market.

Our planes had troubles, so we got another day in London, this time staying at our officer's club. The boys who were new wanted to see the sights and arose early, but I sacked it away until completely rested and then went knocking around.

Just across from the club is the bookstore where I bought all my books while in England. The manager remembered me when I dropped in, he even remembered the books I bought and hoped I would come in again. You can't beat the English.

---

96 Billets were soldiers' lodgings in a non-military setting, like a private home or public housing.
97 The "blackout" in London was the blacking out of lights in homes, businesses and public buildings, in order to hinder German efforts to bomb the city at night. Source: www.Primaryfacts.com
98 Piccadilly Circus in London is a circular road junction in the West End (theater district) of London, located over a major tube/subway station. It is a major tourist attraction, and during World War II, many of the servicemen's clubs were located in the area, making it a magnet for many prostitutes. Source: www.Londontopia.net
    Editor's Note: In the first edit of Bud's letters, his mother, Edith, took out the section on the women working in Piccadilly, as she regarded the subject as too scandalous to be included in the collection. In the interest of preserving Bud's full and honest recollections of his wartime experience, however, this section has been reinstated by the editor.

The people seemed unusually cheery and friendly and as this was Saturday P.M. with a bank holiday on Monday there was quite a gay spirit in the air.

The streets were crowded with girls of all sizes and shapes though the potato sack design predominated. English babes still don't have much chique I'm afraid.

Later in the club latrine I noticed a farewell to England written by an American. Very gentlemanly and polite it was with the note of an Englishman thanking him, penned in alongside.

Comparatively few Americans around now.

Noticing an ad for "Hamlet" on the bulletin board I inquired and found John Gielgud[99] to be playing the lead. I caught the matinee.

My interest was doubled because I'd just read the play a month ago as you recall. I was quite carried away for three solid hours. Gielgud was splendid though most of his supporters were quite wooden. Some of those wonderful old lines keep popping into my head at odd moments ever since.

FRANCE

"We Came Straight Over Paris at 9000 Feet "

The next day we took off through the haze for Marseille by way of Paris and Lyon.

The visibility was quite low over England and the channel so that the old "enemy coast" of my combat days appeared slowly

---

99 Sir John Gielgud was one of the most illustrious Shakespearean actors of the 20th Century, (matched only by Sir Laurence Olivier and Sir Ralph Richardson) with a career that continued on for eight decades. His portrayal of "Hamlet" was considered one of the finest of the era, so Bud's timing in catching a performance, in bombed-out London no less, was lucky indeed.

out of the mists as it always did. This time without the welcoming black flak blossoms that used to be thrown across our path.

We came straight over Paris at 9000 feet. Some of the planes went down to 2000 for a better look at the Eiffel Tower, but we kept straight on.

The haze soon cleared away and we could see for miles across the level flat lands of France. I spent a lot of time between K-ration lunches inspecting the villages with their cathedrals and outlying farms. All this with the aid of some powerful binoculars.

At Lyon we turned south and flew down the valley of the Rhone to Marseille.

On our left all the way were the French and Swiss Alps, the first I had seen of them. White peaks 80 miles away seeming to float in a blue sky, their lower part obscured by a line of grey haze. Rising cleanly above them all stood Mt. Blanc[100], 15,000 feet on my map. An impressive sight, much more so than flying right next to Mt. Whitney as we did a month ago. Perhaps I was feeling better—the breakfast may have been better this time.

Of course at a distance mountains take on an other-wordly property not possible at close range where they appear as just a big pile of rock.

Our airport was 15 miles outside Marseille and quite beaten-up by our bombers. We were immediately impressed by the sharp looking hair-do's of the French women. The pilot knew a little French but I knew none and in trying to talk to waitresses on the post I always lapsed into German idiom. For this they smilingly called me "le Boche[101]."

---

100 Mount Blanc, "White Mountain" is the highest mountain peak in the Alps.
101 French wartime slang for a German/obstinate person. From the Latin root word "caput," meaning a head or a head of cabbage. Source: quora.com

The pilot and I took a bus into town which wound past mesas very similar in appearance to the bluffs along the cannonball if I recall correctly. The road was jammed with all kinds of army trucks and jeeps for there are thousands of men camped about the port waiting to go home.

We rumbled by many farms and villas where the family was having its evening meal on long tables under the trees. Many tall wine bottles were on the tables and much good laughter floated up to us as they dined.

In the hills in the outskirts had been built homes and cemeteries resembling pictures of cliff dwellers. The cemeteries were filled with little stone houses in which I presume they placed their dead.

Marseille was crowded with U.S. combat infantry and engineers. All of us agreed we'd never seen a bigger, rougher looking bunch of men in our life, tho they were neat and orderly. They were all so burned by the sun they were as dark as the Latins here and we with our pale faces and summer uniforms stood out like sore thumbs against their olive drab. We felt like 4-f's[102] that night thinking how much hell[103] those guys had been through.

In a small bar near a park my pilot tried out his French on the owner who managed to make us understand he was a bombardier in the last war and was partial to flyers. He backed these doubtful assertions up with vermouth on the house so we didn't investigate too closely.

---

[102] 4F is the military designation given to new registrants who are found to be unfit "for service in the Armed Forces," due to medical, dental, moral or other reasons. Source: www.reference.com

[103] Interestingly, despite the horror of the high casualty rate the Koltun crew experienced while serving in the 492nd Bomb Group, Bud and the boys were still humbled by the sight of the war-toughened infantrymen they encountered in France in the last months of the war. Bud's stoic "keep moving forward" attitude towards his service in the US Army Air Corps is a large part of what got him through the experience and seems to be a common theme among the veterans of the conflict.

After an hour or two in a sidewalk café we came home before (it was dark). We hadn't been out in quite a while and were all beginning to feel it.

Bud's travels with the ATC continued, as the crew continued on to Tripoli in North Africa

TRIPOLI

"You Have the Maps and Can Let Your Imagination Run Away"

Early the next morning we lifted out over the great harbor and across the blue Mediterranean Sea to Tripoli.

A nice thing about being navigator is that you have the maps and can let your imagination run away when you see those ancient coastlines, cities and seas named on the map before you.

I really couldn't see much difference in color between the inland sea and the ocean. It was very calm which caused trouble when I tried to read drift on the waves.

We came over Tunis, Africa but looked in vain for the ruins of Carthage[104]. Too high I reckon.

At Tripoli I was much too tired to do anything but go to bed and save up strength for the next stop.

---

104 Carthage was the capital of the ancient Carthaginian civiliation. It was located on the east side of the Lake of Tunis. Source: www.Wikipedia.org

The ATC "itinerary" from Tripoli to Cairo, in Bud's unique scrawl.

History was made on a daily basis during the storied end of the World War II era. In this next section, Bud mentions the first use of the atomic bomb, an event that changed the world in ways we are still attempting to understand.

Here, Bud gives us his view on life in Egypt in the 1940s, and his observations are acute. He writes of his experiences there with the innocence of the young yank that he was, encountering a wondrous place with an unfailing native optimism. Bud's innate curiosity, so evident here, saw him through many an odd encounter with Egyptian life, circa 1945 (and through the rest of his life as well).

EGYPT

*"I Think They Wait For Men to Get Off The Bus
With a Bewildered or Indecisive Look"*

The next day we flew along the desert rim of Africa to Cairo arriving in mid-afternoon. That's the trouble with this flying east, no matter when we take off the day is always spent when we arrive. We run out from under the sun speeding its descent.

I had just pointed out to the crew the criss-cross of tank tracks and old trenches that mark El Alemein, when the pilot calls me to put on the earphones. All of us listened with mixed feelings to a broadcast describing the first use of the atomic bomb[105].

---

105 On August 6, 1945, US President Harry Truman ordered the first use of an atomic bomb. The bomb was released over the city of Hiroshima in Japan, by the US bomber Enola Gay. The controversial bombing was said to be carried out in response to information suggesting that an American military invasion into Japan would lead to massive American casualties. Source: www.History.com.

I gave the pilot a heading so that we flew in right over the pyramids about 7 miles south west of Cairo.

The view of the pyramids was so well known from pictures that about the only impression I got in our fleeting glimpse was that their pictures hadn't lied. Just beyond them lay the great green ribbon of the Nile valley.

Our field at Cairo was another beautiful A.T.C. base, one of the many that dot the remotest corners of the world. It was in the desert but the ride into the heart of Cairo was only 30 minutes long.

Well of course we went in despite lack of any advice on oriental tricks and deceit or the customs of the merchants to haggle.

On the way in we passed through Heliopolis[106] where we saw our first mosques with their great domes and slender minarets. Parks lined the road where ragged people slept and black robed women nursed their babies, diverting our gaze from the architecture.

Alighting before the Shepard's Hotel in downtown Cairo, we were besieged by guides—"Official Red Cross!" and raggedy kids in dozens trying to sell us knives or leather walking sticks. I think they wait for men to get off the bus with a bewildered or indecisive look and then they pounce. All three of us were as bewildered as they come and somehow found ourselves in a taxi with a large one-eyed, red fezzed Egyptian Dragoman or guide.

In an interesting twist, Bud's future brother-in-law, Will Siri, was a notable biophysicist, environmentalist and mountaineer who also worked as part of the Manhattan Project team from 1943 to 45. The research conducted by The Manhattan Project (headed up by Robert Oppenheimer of the Los Alamos Laboratory) lead to the development of the first atomic bomb. www.wikipedia.org

106 Heliopolis was a major city in ancient Egypt as well as a center of religious life there. Currently it is located in a suburb of Cairo. Source: wikipedia.org

As G.B. Shaw[107] said "The Lord looks after drunks, fools and the United States." He certainly looked after us cause we had an honest guide, one of the few. He took us to an excellent bazaar deep in the native quarter where the Red Cross trades. (We met the girls there the next day.)

NATIVE QUARTER

"Money is Nothing, Only to Be Spent," He Kept Saying

The smell in the native quarter is not too bad, about like a barnyard. The people have the same smell and I didn't find it bad.

This bazaar was off the main drag on a narrow side street (the street of gold).

There was just room for one carriage to move and the place was lined with shops. Most of them were just stalls with the goods displayed on racks, except for the gold jewelry which was protected by glass cases.

We were glad to see many native policemen around cause it was quite a melee of yelling kids (cussing in American), fezzed[108] merchants urging us to their shops and cold eyed men who just looked at us. Our guide, a big burly man, cussed at them in Egyptian and we finally took refuge in the bazaar.

---

107 The often-quoted George Bernard Shaw was a highly influential critic and playwright, who wrote from the 1880s until his passing in 1950. His stage plays, including "Major Barbara" and "St. Joan" are still performed today. His play "Pygmalion" became the book for the landmark, long-running Broadway hit, "My Fair Lady," which starred Julie Andrews and Rex Harrison in its initial run.

108 A fez is a red felt hat traditionally worn in the Balkans. The hat style originated in the Ottoman empire, but later became popular as a luxurious type of headwear in the US during the early 20th Century. Source: www.wikipedia.org

As is the custom we were seated in the quiet rear of the shop and served refreshments. A very delicious Persian tea especially took our fancy. The owner was a smooth boy and was soon rubbing perfume on the back of our hands and giving us the works. "Money is nothing, only to be spent" he kept saying.

I got Jean[109] some perfume and picked a purse for you. It was a chummy little shop, rich with fine goods and incense.

Darkness had fallen by the time we left to visit a nearby mosque with our packages in hand.

On the steps we paused to put slippers over our shoes that our pagan feet might not soil this temple.

We padded through a long passage and then came into an open courtyard that had a dome at one end. In the center of the court was a fountain under a wooden pavilion at which the worshippers must wash before prayer. Along the wall of the court was the usual ornate stonework and looking down into the court was the minaret, its spire now standing out against the stars.

We were quickly ushered out as the place was closing, but from the guide's broken English I gathered a little about the religion.

ISLAM

"Ad-Libbing On The Prayer Is Encouraged"

Moslems must pray five time a day in the mosque whenever the call to prayer goes out from the minaret. Working men are excused if they are busy and may take the prayer in the evening for the day, but rich men or idle ones sin if they do not do

---
[109] Jean was Bud's sister, Jean Siri. Jean was a noted environmental activist and the wife of Will Siri.

the five. Only 8% can read so the service consists mostly of the priest, who has a good voice, sort of chanting passages from the Koran.

In the entrance I saw a bundle of living rags counting on some beads that looked like a rosary. The guide showed me that the string has 99 beads with 3 divisions, 33 to each part. A Moslem takes the first bead in his fingers and says "Allah is God" 33 times moving up one bead each time; then "Mohommed is His prophet" 33 times, etc.,… he said ad-libbing on the prayer is encouraged.

HAGGLING

"We Met a South African War Correspondent"

The next day at the Shepard's we met a South African war correspondent. He was a charming fellow and gave us many tips on how to get along in the orient, including some suggestions on how to get out of a bazaar with any money left.

By this time we were getting checked out on the art of haggling. The street peddlers invariably ask 3 or 4 times what you should pay but the uninitiated pay. We all had a lot of fun trying to get a bargain. I bought a buffalo horn shoe horn (very useful) for ½ a pound and the peddlers first price was 2 ½ pounds. The ancient art of compromise you know. An Englishman later told me he'd pay a pound for the same shoe horn.

These Egyptian women were quite intriguing, we saw some that could have modeled for statues in the ancient tombs. Most of them were not veiled but wore hot black robes over their heads and often a lot of gold bangles on the forehead. The ones we saw, even the poorer ones certainly had it on the French.

FLIGHT TO IRAN

"Palestine Looked Like Western North Dakota. Only a Little Worse"

After two nights in Egypt we took off and headed northeast across the Suez Canal[110], around the south east corner of the sea, and into the holy land.

In about 2 hours we covered Moses' route of 40 years. Of course he didn't come by the direct scenic route as we did.

Palestine looked like western N. Dak. Only a little worse. The land had very sparse vegetation and was quite hilly.

Jerusalem was on a high plateau only 6 miles to the left of course so we edged over a bit for a look.

We could see its towers and minarets as needle-points when we were 30 miles away. They seemed to be on a level with us because they were on a plateau and the illusion was heightened by the curve up the earth around which we were creeping.

Bethlehem was almost a part of Jerusalem; their suburbs adjoined. We circled once and continued on over the river Jordan with the dead sea on our right. The Jordan Valley was 1000f feet below sea level where we crossed.

On most of these hops we fly at about 8 to 10,000 feet so coast lines look pretty much like the map and little detail in the topography can be seen.

---

110 The Suez Canal is an artificially created waterway in Egypt. It connects the Mediterranean Sea to the Red Sea, by way of the Isthmus of Suez. It officially opened in 1869. The canal allows for a much shorter trip between the North Atlantic and northern Indian Oceans. Source: wikipedia.org

For hours we flew east following the great pipeline across the desert to the valley of the Tigris and Euphrates. We passed in sight of a cluster of mud huts called Bagdad and over the site of ancient Babylon.

How the mighty have fallen! That great valley, tho it had a little green to it, was covered by a dust cloud which rose 9,000 feet in the air and in which we flew all the way to the Persian Gulf.

At the mouth of the Tigris and Euphrates we landed. The town was called Abadam[111], one of the ports that kept the Russians going.

This spot is really the end of creation. The temperature frequently gets up to 180 degrees F. tho it was only 120 the day we were there. A continual dust haze fills the air, so thick it is dangerous for planes to land in the late afternoon. The wind is right off the desert and is so hot and dry that despite the heat we got a chill when covered with sweat we stepped out of the plane into that furnace—instantly drying off.

Fortunately the officers club was air-conditioned for the barracks were intolerable despite an 8 inch matting roof and crude cooling system.

The heat wilted the most ambitious men and everyone just sat in the club and dozed.

My pilot, being a very garrulous fellow, fell in with some Indian officers and we spent the evening together, talking while the atmosphere cooled enough to sleep.

These Indians were big boys, black as pitch, but with cultured English voices. They are treated by the British as we treat our negroes and they were a little bitter. Our friendliness thus pleased them all the more.

---

111 Abadam is a local government area located on the western coast of Lake Chad in Nigeria.

Bud's hand-scrawled ATC itinerary for the trip from Calcutta to Karachi.

ON TO INDIA

*"We Followed The Route of Alexander The Great...
A Tough Place To Walk."*

The next day, in a continual haze, and for the first time since I started navigating, with no wind at all for several consecutive hours—We flew down the Persian Gulf and along the south coast of desolate, rugged Iran—Into Karachi India.

We followed the route of Alexander the Great[112] along the Persian coast, a tough place to walk.

I'm certainly getting enough views of desert and ocean this trip. From Tripoli to India only 3 small strips of green to break the monotony of grey sand hills.

KARACHI

"We All Got a Laugh Out of the Pained Dignity of the Camels."

Karachi is a large port on the west coast about 80 (or 60?) miles north of the mouth of the Indus river. They told us it was the cleanest town in India though you couldn't prove it without a heavy bribe.

On the ride into town we all got a laugh out of the pained dignity of the camels, but we really couldn't blame their expression for they were hauling manure. They have bells on their knees which jingle as they walk, adding to their lugubriousness.

---

112 Alexander the Great was the ruler of the ancient kingdom of Macedon in ancient Greece, and is considered one of the most successful military leaders in all of history. He lead military campaigns in Asia and northeast Africa, and by the age of 30, he had created an empire that stretched from Greece to northwestern India. Source: www.Wikipedia.org/wiki/Alexander_the_Great

Hindus served us in the officer's club and none of us have had such service before. Never was a glass empty or a plate bare. They watched us like hawks and extremely quick and courteous.

As in Egypt—If you are in the shopping district and stop or walk too slow on the street you are besieged by street peddlers selling knives, contact men for boot shops, kids selling the usual "feelthy" stories and men and women beggars in their rags. The people were much more courteous and likeable than in Egypt and looked just like white men except for their dark skin.

NATIVE SHOPS

"Jackson From Chicago"

To shake the pack we hired a little boy, who called himself "Jackson from Chicago" and was full of American slang, to take us to a good shop. We went by horse-drawn carriage to which one of the beggar women hung on as we trotted away. She ran for a block and a half calling for something for her starving baby. All three of us dug like mad after we'd let her run a while, thinking she would let go, but she wouldn't till we gave in. We were afraid of giving anything to beggars because of the way they gang up on a generous guy.

In little stalls along the streets native craftsmen, tailors, shoemakers, etc…, turn out their products while the sacred cows wander around untended among the crowds. The beggars digging among the refuse dumps are a pitiful lot, in rags and tatters, some horribly deformed. There is a lot of T.B. of the bone here besides everything else you could think of.

The better shops had beautiful goods and were as nice inside as anything we have. The owners were the only fat Indians we saw. In these good shops you can't do very much haggling, at which we were getting adept by this time.

The guys I did haggle with got a lot of fun out of the transaction and so did I. one of them took place in "cheap John's place" with John himself. "Very nice ivory, how much?" I ask. "30 rupees ($9.)," says John. "Very nice but too much money, see this flaw, now give me a price," I say. "26 rupees, I see you like it so I'm giving you a price, I like to do business with you." I say "Still too much." So he says "Well I see you like it, I don't want to make money, just do business, you want it, how much will you give? If you name a price that gives me its cost you can have it."

I smile and hem and haw, you can't go too low or its no deal—finally I say 20 rupees. "Take it, take it, you want,--20 rupees" he gasps with resignation. He made plenty at that.

When I ran out of money I haggled for the other guys.

HINDU RELIGION

"One Clerk Told Me The Story Of This God"

I liked the Indians very much and talked quite a bit with some of the clerks—about their education and religion. One of the ivory items that will go good on the mantle is the Hindu god Ganesha (Pronounced Gunish). He is the son of Shurya (Shiva) the sun God. This Ganesha is their God of good fortune and has four arms and an elephant's head.

Since I appeared interested one clerk told me the story of this god and all the other clerks eventually joined in.

It seems that Hindu's worship one great god Brahma, but he is so great it would be improper to worship him directly so they get to him through these hundreds of minor gods.

The story goes that Shurya, the sun-god, left his wife one day to go to the woods and hunt. In the meantime the wife got lonesome and fashioned a son out of mud. Then she gave the mud life and called the boy Ganesha.

One day the wife was taking a bath when the little boy came home and tried to open the door. At the same time Shurya, the father, returned from his long hunt and seeing what he thot was an intruder, he whipped out his snickersnee and beheaded Junior with no questions asked.

The wife was cut to the quick by this rash deed, (not to mention Junior) and stormed at the father, telling him he must restore the head. According to the rules, Shurya could take the head of the first thing to pass the city gate after sun-up of the following day and put it on the son. A baby elephant was unlucky enough to amble through the gate first. Thus the weird looking idol I'll be sending home.

At the present time this god resides on Mt. Everest where he contradicts his supposed good nature, by dumping avalanches and other unpleasantness on mountain climbers. "Ah, but the British flew over Mt. Everest 10 years ago" I told them. This was news to them and caused a great commotion until one added with dignity that the gods on Everest commuted between there and heaven. The honor of the gods was untarnished.

You couldn't question the sincerity of these men, but what a waste that ancient mysticism causes. Starving cattle everywhere and even more starving men, but none will eat. This life is nothing—a burden to be bore for a time and then cast away gladly to enter into the higher existence.

✈

We got off the truck in the center of the town and stepped into an unbarred zoo. One skinny youth had two monkeys that did somersaults and then put a hand on your shoe by way of begging. Another kid had a small black bear that had been de-toothed.

In the center of a circle was a kid of 12 or so blowing on his wooden sweet potatoe and charming two big cobras. I should say he was trying to charm them for they continually struck at him, snapping out of their quivery stance, occasionally they got a hit. We couldn't tell whether they had been defanged or not but it was quite exciting anyway. Cobras are beautiful snakes, glistening like polished steel as they fold and unfold their hood.

The snakes seemed pretty nonchalant about the whole performance though the charmer was in dead ernest whenever he started to play, and gasped for breath between passages.

By horse-drawn ricksha we got out to the Taj Mahal[113] on the river at the edge of town. We'd seen it as we flew in. You couldn't miss seeing it as the rest of the town is brown and it is pure white.

We'd had so many rave notices on this Moslem shrine that we rather expected to be disappointed but no one was, not even the most cynical—a guy who had been in the ATC for three years and had "seen everything."

---

113 The Taj Mahal, which was completed in 1643, is an all-white mausoleum located in the Indian city of Agra. It is an architectural jewel that symbolizes the rich history of India, and was built at a cost of $827 million in today's dollars. Source: Wikipedia.

The famous view from the entrance gate of the main building at the end of the avenue of trees that stand on either side of a long reflecting pool, was especially striking. We saw the great dome in mid-afternoon, shining in the sunlight with fluffy clouds behind it, the same dazzling white.

In stocking feet we went gaping with the usual guide from whom we learned that the temple is of solid marble and took 20,000 workmen 20 years to build back in 1620. The supervisor was an Italian, but the workers came from China, Italy, and India. It was built by the ruling prince for his wife, and they are both buried inside.

The whole thing is so well built you are just as impressed when you look at the intricate inlay work in odd corners as you are when you see the entire main building and minarets from a distance.

Some of the flower designs inlaid in the marble with precious stones are so good that the flowers are three-dimensional and appear solid enough to touch.

A mile up the river lay the great fortress and palace of the former native princes. As usual we had a guide who had no teeth and talked like it, in addition to having lost his grip on the English language. One of the pilots could almost understand him so with the aid of a double translation we managed.

In this royal home we finally found a splendor that could match Hollywood's version of a royal Indian home.

Best thing about it was a marble balcony above the river from which we had a view of the Taj shining in the sun a mile away on a river bend.

The countryside seemed almost like England. Very lush and green with many hedges and lines of trees dividing the land into tiny plots.

TAKE OFF FROM KARACHI

"On Any Take Off Most People Are a Little Nervous"

This last section of Bud's remembrances of the ATC flights was written later, in his war diary, after he had finally finished his service and returned to North Dakota, as he notes in the preface to this last section.

BUD'S NOTE: (written later after our return to the U.S.)

They filled our C-48 with six tons of freight before we left Karachi and the boxes were piled high right up to my desk. They were all roped down but I knew that a wheels up landing would put them all over me.

We had considerable engine trouble on this trip and had changed spark plugs completely three times; the latest at Karachi.

On any take-off most people are a little nervous and I was more than a little at the thought of all that freight to lift with our Hamilton Standard Propellors. These props were not designed for the plane and necessitated a considerably longer run to become air-borne. The Curtiss-electric props we should have had were all going to the B-29's.[114]

---

114 B-29s were four engine heavy bombers designed by Boeing Aircraft. These bombers were propeller driven and one of the largest aircraft models used during World War II. Source: Wikipedia.

The pilot got in line with the runway, slowly advanced the throttles and down the concrete we rushed. I looked out the window by my desk and saw the ground start to drop away. A sigh of relief almost escaped me—when the left engine began to backfire in a steady stream.

You don't have to have flown very much to realize what that sound would do to the nerves of old aircrew hands like us.

After shedding ten years of my life the engine started purring again and we slowly gained altitude—slowly is right it took 10 minutes to get 1000 feet.

I went up and grinned wanly at the pilot. We decided to go on as everything seemed to be all right now and none of us wanted to make another take-off that wasn't necessary in a plane whose engines acted up.

KARACHI TO AGRA

"Some People Worked on Leather Goods or Smoked; Others Just Sat"

More desert this time and then green country with many flooded rice-fields. Little patches of field with a village in the center of a group.

We landed at Agra in north central India and immediately took off for town past people living in pig sties. Mud everywhere, animals wandering around, among the houses and these wretched bony people sitting on their haunches. Some worked on leather goods or smoked; others just sat. Women, usually with more clothes on than the men, laundered, drew water and sat on their haunches talking.

The air got pretty ripe in that town. Overhead, high and low, buzzards wheeled slowly in great circles. I hope they found what died for something certainly had, and not recently.

These buzzard were so thick that at Karachi they warned us of them as a definite danger to flying. They have been known to become incensed at airplanes and to make diving "kamikaze"[115] attacks, doing fearful damage if they hit the pilot's windshield.

In direct contrast to the usual hollow-eyed wrecks on the streets we saw a regiment of Burkhas[116] march by one day. They looked as sharp as cadets; small handsome men with fine features; clean shaven, and cocky in Australian type hats with the folded brim and battle jackets.

PULITZER'S MAN

"He Didn't Seem Like Any Genius"

We were at Karachi for 39 days and in that time, I got acquainted with a 40 year old captain who slept next to me. We gradually found out we had common reading interests and thus became more friendly. Before I left, we visited town together.

He didn't seem like any genius but it turned out much to my surprise that he was assistant editor to Pulitzer of the "St. Louis Post-Dispatch" and in quite a position of influence, though he didn't say so in that many words.

---

115 Kamikaze attacks were suicide missions by Japanese pilots fighting against Allied naval ships at the end of the Pacific campaign during World War II.
116 "Regiment of Burkhas" here refers to members of the Indian Army, who served during World War II and who, by the end of the war, made up the largest volunteer army in history. At the end of the war British Prime Minister Winston Churchill noted "The unsurpassed bravery of Indian soldiers and officers" who served during the conflict. Source: Wikipedia.

At dinner he told me about how he got in the game and all about Pulitzer.[117] He said that Pulitzer's favorite pastime is hunting ducks although he has only 50% vision in one eye and none in the other. "He aims at the moving blurs."

The army had given the captain quite a bad time because he balked at some of the odious jobs they'd asked him to do, writing for public relations.

VICTORY

"I Got Quite Elated Laying in Bed Thinking of a Discharge"

Victory[118] was received quite calmly here—a few that tried hard enough to find some stuff got drunk—the rest went on sitting, swooshing flies and reading. I got quite elated lying in bed thinking of a discharge and college life again after a long rest with you. I suppose the Atc will be last out though.

LAUNDRY

"The Same As A Man Washing His Car So It Will Rain"

In the Atc if you want to be shipped out of a post in a hurry you send in your laundry. It works the same as a man washing his car so it will rain.

---

117 Joseph Pulitzer was an innovative and highly influential editor and publisher who established the model for the modern newspaper. The prestigious Pulitzer Prize was established by Pulitzer through an endowment to Columbia University. Source: Brittanica .com.
118 Victory—the war had ended, as Japan surrendered, on August 15, 1945

I fearluffly turned the dirty duds in and sure enough—we were sent out the next day before they had a chance to come back.

The war was over. The "Hard Luck Crew" had made it; somehow they had avoided disaster again and again, even as many of the other men they served so closely with met a tragically different fate. Bud had survived his run of missions over Europe with the Koltun crew and had had a daring adventure with the Air Transport Command that took him all across the world. At age 23, Bud was a seasoned war veteran. He would live with his memories of the war and of the brave men with whom he had served for the rest of his days.

Chapter 5

Epilogue

*A*fter the war, Bud returned home to North Dakota as a 23-year-old war veteran, ready to make a plan for the rest of his life. He took advantage of the G.I. Bill, which allowed WW II veterans to attend any college they wished, tuition-free. He decided on Berkeley, which to him was a kind of paradise after the stress of war and the frozen North Dakota winters of his childhood. After Berkeley, he returned to North Dakota to attend medical school, and there he met a poetic young beauty (the daughter of Icelandic immigrants) named Muriel Einarson, who soon became his wife.

Bud finished his medical studies at Northwestern University in Chicago, and then went on to the Mayo Clinic, in Rochester, Minnesota. Eventually, John (Bud) and Muriel and their two young boys, John and Daniel, left Minnesota and headed west where John would become a partner in a new medical clinic in Medford, Oregon.

The Brandenburgs thrived in semi-rural Oregon, where Bud and Muriel welcomed two more children, Molly and Eric, into the family. The Medford Clinic flourished in Southern Oregon, and it sparked the development of a huge medical community in the area. Along with creating a legacy as a physician, Bud also came into his own as an artist, as he discovered that painting gave his creative spirit free reign during his hours off from his medical practice.

EPILOGUE

For his children, Bud's war experience was always a presence, albeit in the background of their family life. We knew of Dad's service, and we were given rules of family life based on principals of mutual respect, sharing and camaraderie that seemed to have been taken from a WW II military handbook.

Always, there was talk of "the letters," Dad's written account of his service in Europe, but we didn't actually have access to his collected writings until mom and dad were in their later years. For me, finally reading the letters was a revelation, as Bud's voice and personality resonate clearly from his writing, even though his impressions of the war had been recorded long before my brothers and I were born.

Bud died in 2005 after a long struggle with Alzheimer's disease. The disease robbed Bud of his memory and his personality, and in a sense he left us years before he passed on physically. As dementia set in for Bud, he often experienced episodes in which he believed he was still in Europe bunking with his fellow crew members, gearing up for missions in the fight against the Nazis. The trauma of the war had clearly always been with him, and it manifested again as his illness took away his ability to exert control over his thoughts and emotions.

Even still, Bud left behind a great legacy through his work as a physician in Southern Oregon and by his efforts in laying down a foundation for the area's thriving medical community.

For me, working to re-edit these letters has provided deep and unexpected healing. It is our family's hope that these letters will give the reader a strong sense of who Bud was as an individual, as well as who he was as a soldier who served with the Allies in their historic fight for democracy.

Ultimately, Bud was a yank who didn't hesitate to fight with valor and commitment, and he left behind a great contribution through service to his community, his family, and to his country.

"So it came to pass that as he trudged from the place of blood and wrath his soul changed. He came from hot plowshares to prospects of clover tranquility, and it was as if hot plowshares were not. He had rid himself of the red sickness of battle. He had been an animal blistered and sweating in the heat and pain of war. He turned now with a lover's thirst to images of tranquil skies, fresh meadows, cool brooks—an existence of soft and eternal peace."

—*The Red Badge of Courage,* by Stephen Crane

Bud's portrait during his time as a Doctor of Internal Medicine in Medford, Oregon.

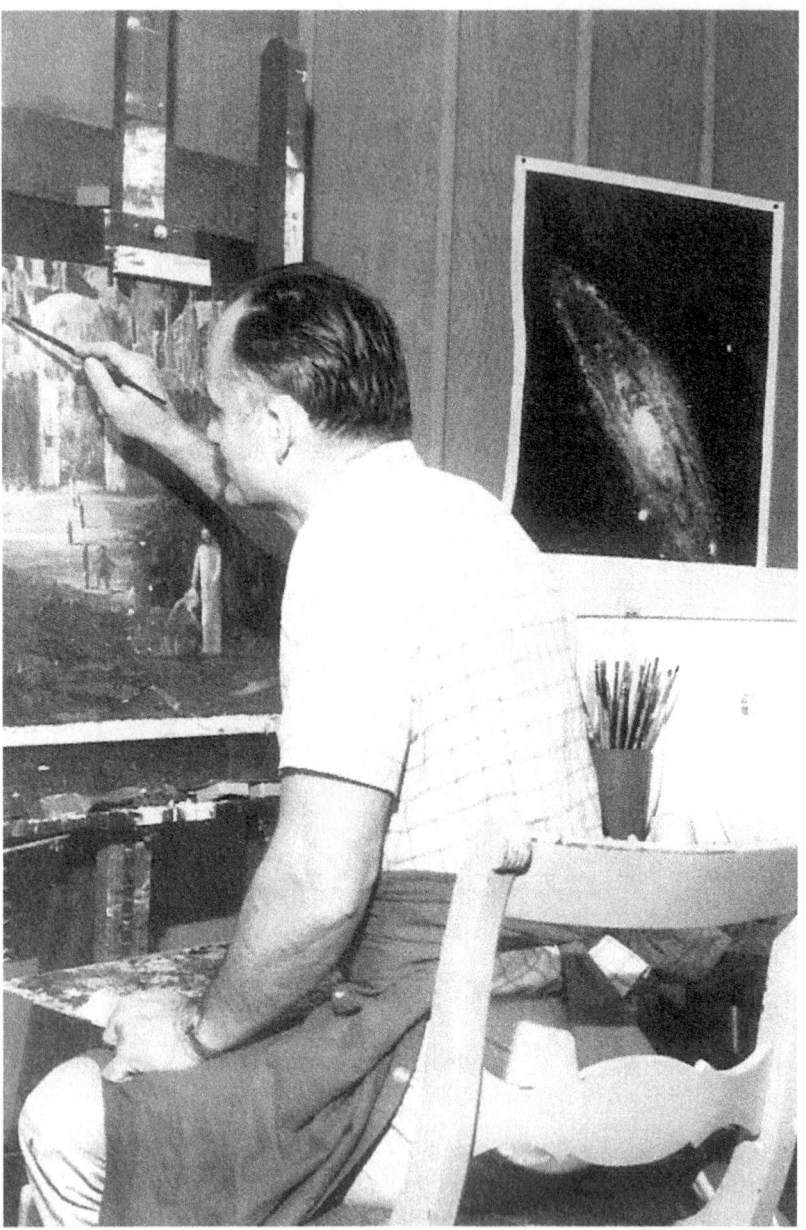

Bud in his art studio, embracing the creative life in the years after the war.

Bud's natural charisma shone especially bright in dress uniform.

Chapter 6

The Koltun Crew Log Book

The experience of joining the war was obviously a life-changing event for the young men of the World War II era. Many of these men took a look around and realized they were involved in something that was much bigger than themselves and this recognition inspired many of them to record their reflections on their day-to-day service in the war in any way they could. For these men, writing about their experiences gave them a sense of perspective on what they were seeing and feeling, as well as a chance to share those feelings with their families back home.

Along with Bud's written observations, the Koltun crew record also includes entries from a mission log book kept by another member of the crew. The young man who wrote the log recorded his observations of the events that took place during each mission, along with technical details regarding the flights. These observations provide a parallel yet more sober narrative of the wartime events observed by Bud, and we have included the Log Book in order to give readers another perspective on the events of the war. The log begins as the crew members make their initial journey to Europe to begin their service with the Allied Forces.

The log is presented as recorded, with no edits except where needed for clarity.

THE LOG BOOK

LOG BOOK OF THE 14ᵀᴴ WING WITH THE 44ᵀᴴ & 32ᴺᴰ GROUP
857ᵀᴴ BOMB SQUADRON, 492ᴺᴰ BOMB GROUP

CREW #718
HUT #16
SITE 1

STATISTICS

We used 22 different numbered planes to fly our 30 missions.

TWO IN 385X
NINE IN 118V

ONE EACH

313A	021B	258H
23OR	091F	340B
177Q	121T	247H
0230	158K	526R
171Z	211V	308Q
989	115U	324S
220H		

We destroyed 165,000 lbs. of assorted bombs or 820 Tons in all 30 missions.

Average bombing for all 30 missions was 24,400 ft. Lowest bombing for one mission was at 14,500 ft. and the highest was 16,000 ft.

LOG BOOK ENTRY DATE: April 20, 1944

We test hopped our new plane at Mitchel Field and flew over New York for about two hours. We buzzed the pilot's house in Brooklyn and the plane responded perfectly to all the maneuvers that the pilot put it thru. Back at the base, our plane ran off the runway as it was being parked. No damage resulted and it was pulled out with a cleat track.

DATE: April 21, 1944

We loaded all our baggage in the plane and we all took turns in standing guard until take off the following morning.

DATE: April 21, 1944

The weather was clear and we took off in the morning for Bangor, Maine (Dow Field). We flew around the Statue of Liberty and the heart of New York before heading out on course. On the way out we saw New York in grand style and also Coney Island. We landed at Bangor, Maine during the afternoon and had everything taken care of before leaving the states.

DATE: April 23, 1944

Our plane broke thru the runway before take off and had to be pulled out. We took off shortly before noon and landed at Goose Bay, Labrador some 4 ½ hrs later.

On the way out we flew over the St. John River that divides the States from Canada at that point. We also flew over the Gulf of St. Lawrence which is very picturesque. We didn't have any trouble finding the field and landed with snow banks six feet on both sides of the runway. About 20 planes landed and the weather was very cold all thru our stay which was three days. We didn't do anything except wait for our next move.

DATE: April 26, 1944

We took off shortly before mid-nite from Goose Bay for Meeks Field, Iceland. This place is about 30 miles from Reykjavik, a modern city and it's heated by hot water coming from the ground. Our trip was during the night and because of 3 & 4 hours of darkness, they only get this time of year. We had lights most of the time, we flew just below the Northern lights at one time. One time we flew blind because of the clouds and the temperature was around 21 below. When we reached Iceland, the undercast was so thick we had to fly in that vicinity for about two hours before being called in. The wind was terrific when we landed and blew most of the time during the winter months, we stayed here for four days. Our trip took over nine hours.

✈

DATE: April 31, 1944

We left Meeks Field, Iceland for Nutts Corner, Ireland, during the morning and got there some 5 hrs. later. Ireland from the air looked very beautiful with its hedges, all the way thru the country side. We left our planes there, which was going to be flown to some modification center. This was the last time we've saw the plane that brought us across. Nutts Corner is about 27 miles from Belfast. We only stayed here for a day and a half and were on the move once more.

DATE: May 1, 1944

We left Nutts Corner by truck during the afternoon and drove 12 miles to a station, where we boarded a train for Larne, Ireland. We stayed at Larne overnight, which was a camp for the British. Food was terrible and here we slept on board with only a straw mat for a mattress. It was very cold and damp.

✈

DATE: May 2, 1944

Our group left Larne, Ireland during the morning by Ferry Boat. The trip took us about 3 hrs into Stranraer. We walked to a British camp about a miles from the dock and waited for a train. We boarded the train and rode all night until we arrived at Stone, England. We stayed at a place called Nelson Hall which was previously occupied by women war workers. We stayed here to wait for further orders.

DATE: May 9, 1944

We left Stone, England during the afternoon train and got into Stranrear, Scotland early the next morning. The following morning we went to a British camp and we slept there and the beds were horrible.

DATE: May 10, 1944

We took the ferry back for Larne, Ireland. Here, we boarded a train and arrived at a place called Cookstown, Ireland during the night. We registered at a place called Cluntoe and then were driven to a place called Green Castle some 70 miles away.

DATE: May 11, 1944

We stayed here for only a few days and then flew back to Green Castle which only took a half an hour.

✈

DATE: May 13, 1944

From 15th to 18th, we attended school at Cluntoe. After that we flew back Thursday evening to Green Castle, where we attended school for the following 6 days.

May 18, 1944

From the 19th to the 24th we attended Gunnery school at Green Castle. We left there on the 25th.

May 25, 1944

We left Green Castle during the afternoon and drove some distance and boarded a train for Larne. We stayed there for the night and the following day took the ferry for Stranrear, Scotland. We stayed there for 5 hours and then got on a train and reached our permanent base, Saturday May 27, 1944 at PICKENHAM, ENGLAND.

✈

The author of the log book (unfortunately his work was not signed, so we do not know which crew member recorded these notes) also made this overview of the crew's duties and the missions flown.

From the Log:

NOTES

The duty of the Radio man besides being a radio operator was to release the bombs manually from the bomb bay on signal.

PLACES STATIONED: 8th Air Force 442nd-445th

Westover Field, Mass
Mitchell Field, New York
Bangor, Maine
Goose Bay, Labrador
Meeks Field, England
Nutts Corner, England
Nelson Hall, Stone, England
Green Castle, England
Cluntoe, Ireland
North Pickenham, England   442nd
Tibenham, England   445th

MISSIONS

Mission	Date
1. ST. AVORD, FRANCE	June 4, 1944
2. Cherbourg Penninsula, France	June 6, 1944
3. Laval, France	June 8, 1944
4. Dreux, France	June 12, 1944
5. Emmerich, Germany	June 14, 1944
6. Tours, France.	June 15, 1944

7. Melun, France	June 17, 1944
8. Wesermunde, Germany	June 18, 1944
9. St. Vinocq, France	June 19, 1944
10. Laon, France	June 23, 1944
11. Peronne, France	June 25, 1944
12. Saarbrucken, Germany	June 28, 1944
13. Madgeburg, Germany	June 29, 1944
14. Kiel, Germany	July 6, 1944
15. Munich, Germany	July 12, 1944
16. Saarbrucken, Germany	July 16, 1944
17. Caen, France	July 18, 1944
18. Oberpfaffenhofen, Germany	July 21, 1944
19. Bremen (Oslebshausen), Germany	July 29, 1944
20. Laon, France	Aug. 1, 1944
MISSIONS	
(2)	
21. Mery sur Oise, France	Aug. 3, 1944
22. Hamburg, Germany	Aug. 6, 1944
23. Ostend, Belgium	Aug. 7, 1944
24. Zwischenahn, Germany	Aug. 15, 1944
25. Granienburg, Germany	Aug. 27, 1944
26. Karlsruhe, Germany	Sept. 8, 1944
27. Ulm, Germany	Sept. 10, 1944
28. Hanover, Germany	Sept. 11, 1944
29. Hanover, Germany	Sept. 12, 1944
30. Ulm, Germany	Sept. 13, 1944
END OF MISSIONS	

— — — — — —

MISSION
(1)

TARGET:	ST. AVORD, FRANCE	AIR FIELD
DATE:	Sunday June 4, 1944	Plane #118-V
TAKE OFF:	15:45	7 hrs 12 mins.
LANDED:	22:57	Oxygen 4 ½ hrs.
BRIEFED:	13:30	Bombs dropped 20:26
BOMB LOAD:	12 – 500 Demolition Bombs	
TARGET BOMBED:		18,000 ft. 8 below

REMARKS:

Flak was very heavy around the coast line and also the target. Our plane wasn't hit. We were escorted by P-47 most of the time over enemy territory. Plane and guns were in perfect working order. Visibility was very good all around the target and one could see the target completely destroyed. One plane was lost on this mission. Visibility was bad at this time & the pilot of lost plane tried to avoid a head on collision and his plane went into a dive and he was unable to pull it out. We flew over London on this mission. Coming back to the base, the field was closed in and some planes had to find shelter at other air bases. It was raining at the time. The usual routine after landing is to get your flying clothes off and go for coffee and sandwiches and then go to the Interrogation room and give details on the mission that was just completed.

Our group had 41 planes.

— — —

INVASION
D DAY

MISSION

(2)

TARGET:	CHERBOURG PENNINSULA, FRANCE – FORT EN BESSIN	
DATE:	Tuesday, June 6, 1944 – Plane #118-V	
TAKE OFF:	03:22	5 hrs. – 30 mins.
LANDED:	08:52	Oxygen 2 ½ hrs.
BRIEFED:	22:30	Monday, June 5 1944
BOMB LOAD:	52 Clusters (312 Bombs, 20 each Fragmentation	
TARGET BOMBED:	06:08 16,000 ft. 12 below	

Our group had every available plane up throughout the day (3 missions)

REMARKS:

The BIG DAY finally came and much excitement was shown when the fellows were told that this was it. We took off on time and shortly after our number one engine caught fire. Nothing serious and went out in a few minutes. As we were waiting for take off, we could see in a distance where a bomber had crashed and the bombs were bursting as the fire continued. Visibility was very bad at the time we were forming our elements. We finally started out for the enemy coastline and one could see bombers in front and behind as far as one could see.

Over the channel it was cloudy one could see boat after boat without let-up. Our Wing Division concentrated on dropped their bombs on a 10 mile beach head around Port en Bessin.

All bombing was to cease at 06:38 for Land Forces were to hit the beach at 06:30. Pathfinders means were used for bombing because we practically flew over the enemy islands of Guernsey and Jersey. We saw a few of our fighters and didn't meet any Fighter opposition.

MISSION

(3)

TARGET:	LAVAL FRANCE
DATE:	June 8, 1944
TAKE OFF:	04:48 Total: 6 hrs – 28 mins
LANDED:	11:16 on oxygen 4 hrs
BOMB LEAD:	12-500 #Demolition bombs
TARGET BOMBED:	at 16,230 ft – 17 below our group had 40 Planes.

REMARKS:

Got up at 8 o'clock & briefed at 2:30. The Weather was fair. Visibility was very bad at the time of take off and we climbed to 22,000 ft. where it was 27 degrees below. Our group was pretty badly split up & we ended up by bombing another target with another group. We were briefed to bomb a Rail Center at Angers, France. So we ended up by bombing an airplane factory, which was completely wiped out. We had fairly good fighter protection and didn't meet any Fighter opposition. No flak on this mission, visibility was fairly good over the target, although returning back to our base, we found the field practically closed in. After making two landing attempts, we finally landed. It was a relief to everyone.

— — — —-

MISSION

(4)

TARGET: DREUX, FRANCE
DATE: Monday June 12, 1944 Plane #118-V
TAKE OFF: 05:19 Total hrs. 6 hrs – 8 mins.
LANDED: 11:27 on oxygen 4 hrs.
BRIEFED: 01:00 – Bombs dropped at 03:37
BOMB LOAD: 24-250 # Demolition bombs
TARGET BOMBED: 20,500 ft. – 18 below
Our group had 36 planes

REMARKS:

We didn't get any sleep. Had lunch at mid-nite & were off for briefing at 01:00. Weather conditions were very good for we didn't have any (trouble) getting into formation with 12 planes in our element. Visibility was exceptionally good over the channel & over enemy territory. Once (we) could see the channel crowded with all types of boats coming and going across. Flak was medium on the way going into the target & was heavy on the way out. We had very little Fighter escort & didn't run into any Fighter opposition, Target was well hit & pictures showed it was completely destroyed.

NOTES

DATE: JUNE 11, 1944

Yesterday, Sunday June 11th. We went on a mission and had to return, because we never found our Lead plane from another group, what were we supposed to bomb with the Pathfinder (PTF). We carried a bomb load of F-1000 Demolition bombs on this mission. After returning back to the base. We landed as usual and this time the brakes failed to hold in order to have the plane come to a stop, so we had to keep on going, off the runway and ended up crossing the road and mired down in a muddy field. They had quite a time to take the live bombs out of the Bomb Bay.

✈

Here the log book author adds an unusual personal aside, adding to the poignance of his notes on the mission:

I REMEMBERED THE ROAD AS SOON AS I SPOTTED IT ON THE WAY TO THE AIR FIELD ON MY RETURNED VISIT TO ENGLAND

NOTES –

(1)
After every briefing, we all stand up and a chaplain leads a prayer* before we start on our mission. This is always done throughout the Air Force. Regardless of where you are stationed.

(2)

Our first mission was the group's sixteenth, the group originally came from Alamogordo, New Mexico and got here the latter part of April. The first missions flown by this group was made on May 11, 1944 to Mulhouse, France. Which is located near the Swiss border.

— — — —-

MISSION

(5)

TARGET:	Emmerich, Germany
DATE:	Wednesday June 14, 1944 Plane #118-V
TAKEOFF:	04:50 Total 4 hrs 35 mins.
LANDED:	09:25 Oxygen 2 ½ hrs
BRIEFED:	00:30 Bombs dropped at 07:27
BOMB LOAD:	250 # Demolition Bombs
TARGET BOMBED:	18,800 ft – 21 below
	Our group had 50 Planes.

REMARKS:

We didn't get any sleep. Had lunch at mid-nite & were off for briefing shortly after. Weather conditions were very good all thru this mission. Our group was split up & half went on a mission to France & the other half into Germany. We were escorted by a large group of P38st & P-47 planes most of the time we were over enemy territory. Very little Flak & no enemy Fighter opposition. Target was well hit & pictures showed tremendous damage. This target is located on the Rhine River & in a fair size city.

— — — —-

MISSION

(6)

TARGET: Tours, France – R.R. Bridge – 5 miles east of Tours
DATE: Thursday June 15, 1944 Plane #230-R
TAKE OFF: 04:25   5 hrs. 44 mins.
LANDED: 10:09   Oxygen 4 hrs.
BRIEFED: 00:45   Bombs dropped at 07:22
BOMB LOAD: 12:500 #demolition bombs
TARGET BOMBED: 20,110 ft – 17 below
Our group had 25 Planes

REMARKS:

We didn't get any sleep, had breakfast at mid-nite & were off for briefing. Weather conditions were very good all the way thru on this mission. We flew over London on the way to the target & one could see balloons well distributed over the London area. We ran into stiff fighter opposition for the first time. Our Squadron only lost one plane & other suffered a much heavier loss. Flak was fairly heavy after we left our target. Our target was a double track Railroad bridge (34 ft. wide – 1200 ft. long) which was located 5 miles East of Tours on the Loire River. The target was completely destroyed by our wing, which consisted of our group the 492th, 392nd, & 44th Bomb Group. After we had bombed we flew over the city & we saw the two bridges which were located in the heart of the city, completely knocked out by the wings that follow us.

MISSION

(7)

TARGET: Melun, France – Air Field
DATE: Saturday June 17, 1944 Plane #177-Q
TAKE OFF: 08:51   - 7 hrs. – 14 mins.
LANDED: 16:05 – Bombs dropped at 13:07
BOMB LOAD: 12-5000 # Demolition Bombs
TARGET BOMBED: 22,000 ft, - 20 below

Our Group had 9 planes out on this mission.

REMARKS:

We got up at 05:30, had no breakfast, had briefing. Visibility not good & we went up to altitude shortly after take off. Flying over the Channel, one could see scores of boats coming and going with war supplies. As we neared the beach head one could see hundreds of boats being unloaded with supplies and men. Visibility was bad over the target & bombing was done by "GH" means. As we neared the target, we hit heavy flak about minute before we dropped our bombs. Three holes were made by Flak to our plane, for the first time on any mission, so far.

MISSION

(8)

TARGET: Wesermunde, Germany – Sub Base
DATE: Sunday June 18, 1944 – Father's Day
TAKE OFF: 05:52 7hrs. 19 mins.
LANDED: 13:02 – oxygen 5 ½ hrs.
BRIEFED: 01:00 – Bombs dropped at 10:42

BOMB LOAD: 40 Clusters (240 bombs-20#each Fragmentation)
TARGET BOMBED: 20,000 19 below
Our group had 36 planes

REMARKS:

We got up a mid-nite after 3 hours sleep. Visibility was fairly good through this mission. We flew over the North Sea on the way going to the target, which took us about two hrs to cross. We touched the coastline of Denmark & circled Hamburg on the way to the target. The lead Navigator used Wilhelmshaven, Germany for a check out point on the way out. Bad mistake, because this place is one of the German Navy Centers(s) and they threw up everything they had at us. We suffered heavy damage. Our plane had 35 holes. Our Element had only 8 planes at the time and ended up by going to the Sub depot for repairs and the other 2 were lost. This was the worst mission so far & it sounded like hail on a tin roof. Our hydraulic system was shot out on the inside of the bomb bays & we were ready with our parachutes in case we had brake failure after landing.

MISSION
(9)

TARGET: St. Vinocq, France – Rocket Installation
DATE: Monday, June 19, 1944 Plane #023-0
TAKE OFF: 07:35   4 hrs. – 5 mins.
BRIEFED: 04:30 – Bombs dropped – 10:41
Landed: 11:30 – On Oxygen 3 hrs
BOMB LOAD: 52-100 # Demolition Bombs
TARGET BOMBED: 21,500 ft – 22 below

Our group had 9 planes

REMARKS:

We got up at 03:30, had lunch and went for briefing. Visibility was very poor throughout the mission and bombing was done by "GH." Results from bombing won't be known until the weather clears & pictures taken of target area. We flew over Belgium on the way going to the target. Flak was light. We brought 10 bombs back because of some mechanical defect that developed with our bomb release.

NOTES

June 20, 21, and 22nd, our crew spent a 48 hour pass in London. On the 29th our group had a mission that took them into Politz, Germany. Our group lost 14 planes on that mission and Lt. Mc Coy and Lt. Kaufmen's crew went down with this group. These two crews were the ones that we trained with in the States and came across with us.

MISSION

(10)

TARGET:	Laon, France – Air Base
DATE:	Friday June 23, 1944 – Plane #171-2
TAKE OFF:	16:28 -5 hrs – 20 mins.
LANDED:	21:38 - oxygen 3 hrs.
BRIEFED:	14:00 – Bombs dropped at 20:02
BOMB LOAD:	52-100 #demolition bombs
TARGET BOMBED:	22, 400 ft, - 19 below
	Our group had 24 planes

REMARKS:

Visibility was fairly good. Fighter protection good. FLAK was very heavy. Our plane suffered a few hits and one went thru the Martin turret without hitting Jacobsen. Our Turret gunner target was well hit and probably put out of commission for a long time. We flew over enemy territory over 2 hours and flew over Holland and Belgium on this mission. Our group lost a few planes because of Flak.

MISSION

(11)

TARGET: Peronne, France – Air Field
DATE: Sunday June 25, 1944 –Plane #989 ?
Take Off: 09:48 – 4 hrs
LANDED: 13:50 on oxygen – 3 hrs.
BRIEFED: 09:00 – bombs dropped at 12:31
BOMB LOAD: 52 – 100 # demolition bombs
TARGET BOMBED: 26,000 ft. 27 below

Our group had 12 planes on this mission

REMARKS:

Weather good, visibility good. We had trouble with our number two engine and debated if we should continue with this mission. High altitude was probably the cause for the plane acting this way, because were flying higher then any other time in the past. We flew over Holland & Belgium on the way to the target. Our plane didn't suffer any hits, the flak was heavy and spotty. Because of our altitude and perfect visibility, we could see a great number of different targets of all sorts, knocked out completely previous to our bombing of today. We could see the

English Shores, which is a distance of 40 miles. The Channel traffic was heavy with our boats & troops back and forth. The Cliffs of Dover could plainly be seen on the way back to our base.

MISSION

(12)
TARGET: Saarbrucken, Germany Marshalling Fields
DATE: Wednesday June 28, 1944 – Plane -071-B
TAKE OFF: 05:49 - 6 hrs.
LANDED: 11:50 - Oxygen 6 hrs
BRIEFED: 02:15 – Bombs dropped at 08:44
BOMB LOAD: 24- 250 # Demolition Bombs
TARGET BOMBED: 22,500 ft. 20 below
Our group had 24 planes

REMARKS:

The weather was partly cloudy & bombing was done with a (PPF) plane. We took off on time & shortly after our plane developed a bad gas leak & had to return back to the base. We got a spare plane & were off again. Our formation was way ahead & we were fortunate in catching it just hitting the enemy coastline. We flew over Holland, Belgium, France & hit the target which is located on the border line between France & Germany. The target was completely surrounded by a smoke screen which covered a great area. Flak was very heavy & our plane suffered many hits. Bryan our nose gunner was hit & lost his index finger.

MISSION

(13)

TARGET: Madgeburg, Germany – Aircraft Works
DATE: Thursday June 29, 1944 – Plane #091 – F
TAKE OFF: 05:45 7 hrs
LANDED: 12:49 Oxygen – 6 hrs
BRIEFED AT: 02:00 Bombs dropped at 09:57
BOMB LOAD: 52 – 100 # Incendiary Bombs
TARGET BOMBED: 22,000 ft. – 21 below

REMARKS:

Weather good, visibility good. We flew over the Frisan Islands, Holland, Belgium. France and Germany on this mission. Flak at the enemy line. The target, Madgeburg is on the River Elbe & was completely surrounded by a smoke screen at the time of the bombing & flak was very thick. Our plane suffered a few bad hits, with the hydraulic system hit for the second time in the bomb bays.

MISSION

(14)

TARGET: Kiel, Germany – Submarine Base
DATE: Thursday July 6, 1944 – Plane "118-V
TAKE OFF: 06:17 6 hrs. 14 mins.
LANDED: 12:31 Oxygen 4 ½ hrs.
BRIEFED AT: 02:31 Bombs dropped at 09:44
BOMB LOAD: 6 – 500 # Demo. & 6 cluster (660-4 ea) Incendiary
TARGET BOMBED: 22,400 ft – 18 below

REMARKS:

The weather was very favorable at the time of take off. Our formation formed at 15,000 ft. and gained bombing altitude on the way to the target. Our group lead the entire wing to the target & we flew the lower left in our element. We didn't suffer any fighter attack, although our upper turret man saw one of our fighters bag one of the enemy fighters on the way going to the target. Visibility poor, had to use the pathfinder (PFF) for bombing the target. Flak was very heavy because of the importance of the target, submarine base withal of its construction around it. We were lucky to be flying in the position we were. For the pattern of the flak was very effective & many planes suffered heavy damage. Our plane was hit 5 times. We flew over the North Sea both coming and returning. The trip over water took about an hour each way.

NOTES

July 7, 8 and 9th our crew spent a 48 hr pass in London. On the 7th, our group had a mission that took them into Bernberg, Germany. Our group lost 12 planes on this mission and Lt. Kilpatrick's crew went down with this mission. They were a crew that trained with us at Westover and came over with us.

July 7, 8 and 9th our crew spent a 48 hr pass in London. On the 7th, our group had a mission that took them into Bernberg, Germany. Our group lost 12 planes on this mission and Lt. Kilpatrick's crew went down with this mission. They were a crew that trained with us at Westover and came over with us.

––––––––

MISSION

(15)

TARGET: Munich, Germany

DATE: Tuesday July 12, 1944 – Plane #118-V

TAKE OFF: 09:31 – 8 hrs. 15 mins.

LANDED: 17:46 – oxygen 6 ½ hrs.

BRIEFED: 06:00 – Bombs dropped at 13:47

BOMB LOAD: 6 – 500 # demo. And 4 cluster – (110 -4) incendiary

TARGET BOMBED: 24,000 ft – 20 below

Our group had 24 planes

REMARKS:

We took off & flew thru an over cast & formed with the lead element at 12,000 ft. We flew over the North Sea, Holland Belgium and Germany. We flew within 29 miles of the Swiss border. We hit flak on the way to the target. We were briefed to hit a target 5 miles east of Munich, which was an Air Base. The over cast was too heavy & we had to drop our load on the secondary target, which was the city of Munich. Yesterday our group hit the same target, which is very unusual to hit the same target two days in a row. Flak was very, very, very heavy at the target and we were lucky not to get hit. We half circled shortly after we dropped our bombs & one could see the heavy concentration of flak over the target, area of 7 to 8 hundred smoke puffs made by the flak. The 8th Air Force had 12,000 heavies out on this mission. We were over enemy territory 5 hrs. On this mission we got a new nose gunner to replace Bryan.

NOTES

Wednesday July 13, 1944 we were slated for a mission into Saarbrucken, Germany. We took off as usual and when it came to raising the landing gear, it refused to work. The pilot called the field and was informed to land at some other field in southern England. Our field closed shortly after we took off because of bad weather. We flew about 25 miles over the North Sea in order to drop our bombs. All bombs are dropped safe in any case like this which often times happens. We landed at this Emergency field, which is located in Manston, England. This field had the largest runway that any of us have ever seen.

— — — — — — — —

MISSION
(16)

TARGET:	Saarbrucken, Germany – Marshalling Yards
DATE:	Sunday July 16, 1944 – Plane # Plane 121 –T
TAKE OFF:	05:56 - 6hrs.
LANDED:	12:23 Oxygen 5 hrs
BRIEFED:	02:15 Bombs dropped at 09:44
BOMB LOAD:	12 – 500 # demolition bombs
TARGET BOMBED:	21,000 ft. – 16 below Our group had 24 planes

REMARKS

Weather good, visibility good. Altho over enemy territory it was partly cloudy & we bombed with the pathfinder because of the overcast that hung around the target. This was the second time we hit this target, because of the great importance as a rail center which was the hub for supplying supplies for France & Italy from Germany. We hit a little flak shortly after we got into enemy territory. Flak was very heavy around the target & we were lucky enough to be slightly to its right so we didn't suffer too much flak. The 8th Air Force hit several other targets in France and Germany. On today's bombing one could see scores of bombers going in different directions over enemy territory. This makes our 16th mission on July 16th.

MISSION

(17)

TARGET:	Caen, France – (Enemy gun installations, etc.)
DATE:	Tuesday July 18, 1944 – Plane #158 M
TAKE OFF:	04:27 4 hrs 16 mins
LANDED:	08:43 Oxygen 3 hrs
BRIEFED:	01:00 Bombs dropped at 07:01
BOMB LOAD:	52 – 100 # Demolition Bombs
Target BOMBED:	14,500 ft. – 10 below

REMARKS:

We didn't get any sleep. Had lunch at mid-nite & was off for briefing. The weather was clear and the sky was filled with stars which was good to see after having it cloudy most of the time. The plane we flew was a "J" series, which has the side windows open instead of the usual Flex windows that all "H" series planes have. We took off as usual, with the Pilot having a little trouble with prop. wash after take off. We didn't have much trouble finding our lead element and got the formation underway. Soon after take off we flew over London area and could see hundreds of balloons scattered all over for their protection from enemy dive bombs and also from the present flying bomb threats that Germany has started some six weeks ago. We bombed a section which is located 4 miles East of Calen and about 5 to 6 miles in from the coastline. The main purpose for this bombing was to help the British and Canadian land forces for further advances which they were up against because of strong Germany opposition in this section. We were over enemy territory for only five minutes. The Germans threw up every thing they had, which was as rough as any other long mission we've had so far...I certainly enjoyed this mission, for one could see the real "McCoy" of war. Gun fire seemed to be all over, with the battle smoke all over the Caen area, which is in the mist of a great Battle. My hat's off to the boys that were fighting below, for it looked like Hell to me without any let up. One could see five or better landing strips already built since we've taken over the Cherbourg Peninsula which are now being used by our Fighter planes. The Channel was just loaded with our boats and I would say there were at least 2000 of them that were doing their part for the War.

MISSION
(18)

TARGET: Oberpfaffenhofen Field Germany – 15 miles from Munich
DATE: Friday July 21, 1944 Plane# 115-7
TAKE OFF: 06:07   7 hrs. 37 mins.
LANDED: 13:44 oxygen – 6 hrs.
BRIEFED: 02:30   Bombs dropped at 10:34

BOMB LOAD: 52-100 # Incendiary Bombs
TARGET BOMBED: 24,000 ft. – 21 – below
                  Our group had 24 planes

REMARK:

We took off as usual & had a little trouble with the prop wash just after leaving the ground. We flew right wing on the lead element & formed at 16,000 ft. We flew over the North Sea, Holland, Belgium & Germany. Flak was fairly heavy in places before we ever hit the target. Visibility was just fair and clouds were as high as 24,000 ft. in places which made formation flying difficulty. Our target was an aircraft factory, that had been hit previous to this. One main section remained, so this was our target, which was hit by us according to reports. Flak was very heavy around target because of it being around the Munich area. We weren't hit by any flak which is always good news. Our bomb load on this mission is the worse one and we always sweat it out when we reach our target. Our Navigator released the bomb load & ten failed to drop.

Two of the bombs jammed the control cables on the inside of the bomb bays and the plane started to drop on its accord. Murphy and Grab left their stations in the waist and freed the cables by removing the two bombs. Grab kicked the two bombs out, plus two more that were hanging loose while Murphy held the bomb bay doors open. The remaining six they toggled out as we were leaving Germany. Shortly after we dropped our bombs, three enemy ME-109 Fighters showed up and bagged one of our bombers, that was flying to our rear. It wasn't long before six of our P-31's showed up and took after them which was a sure kill for them. This was a very tiresome mission for us for we were over enemy territory close to five hours.

NOTES

On July 22, 1944 – July 28, 1944 the crew got a seven day leave. Grab and I spent our leave at Southport, England and the others went elsewhere. We had a grand time with plenty of rest, which was the main reason for our leave. Southport is a vacation center like we have in the States. We stayed at the Palace Hotel which was taken over by the Red Cross since the war was started. Everything was just perfect and we found Southport the nicest City in England so far.

NOTES

August 1944. Our entire group was broken up and Crews went as replacement all over the Second Division. We were the only crew that ended up with the 445th bomb Group. We left our base shortly after supper and got there within an hour by truck. This Group was in the Second Combat Wing with the 453rd and 389th Group. The base was near a town called Tibenham.

— — — — — — — —

MISSION
   (19)

    TARGET: Bremen, Germany (Oslebshausen)
                            Oil Refinery
    DATE: Saturday July 29, 1944 Plane # 118-V
    TAKE OFF: 06:29   6 hrs 16 mins.

LANDED:	12:45	Oxygen 4 ½ hrs
BRIEFED:	02:30	Bombs dropped at 10:07
BOMB LOAD:	16 – 250 # Demo Bombs +	
	4 Incendiary -110 Clusters	
TARGET BOMBED:	23,000 ft 24 below	
	Our group had 30 planes.	

REMARKS:

After getting back from our leave, we managed to get a couple of hours sleep for the past few nights because the first was spent on a train. After briefing we took off. Weather good at take off. We got into our assigned formation and took off for the target about an hour & half after take off. We flew over the North Sea most of the time on this misson. We were over enemy territory for only forty minutes. Flak was intense around the target and bombing was by PFF because of the heavy over cast around the target area. A quarter piece of flak entered thru the Pilot's side window and the breaking of the window was the only damage that resulted from the flak. We had good P-51 Fighter protection and didn't see any enemy aircraft coming back to our base. Bad weather had set in and left visibility practically zero for landing. We finally landed after flying three or four hundred feet during the time we were circling our field and waiting for an opportunity to land. This is the second time our field was practically closed when we got back from a mission, which is suicide flying under such conditions at any time. The Target we bombed was a suburb of Bremen, which is located five miles North West of it.

Reports revealed that the bombing of this target has been the best that our group has ever taken part in.

MISSION

(20)

TARGET:	Leon, France Railroad Bridge
DATE:	Tuesday August 1, 1944 – Plane #211-7
TAKE OFF:	12:21 5 hrs. 32 mins.
LANDED:	17:53 Oxygen 4 hrs
BRIEFED:	06:30
BOMB LOAD:	8-1000 # Demolition Bombs
TARGET BOMBED:	22,000 ft – 16 below
	Our group had 36 planes

REMARKS:

The CQ forgot to wake us up for this morning's mission altho after the Officers got to the assigned plane they didn't find us there and then got the ball rolling. A Sergeant came after us in a jeep and found us still in bed. We were taken to the drying room where we picked up our flying clothes and then were off for our plane. Take off was at 10:00 and was postponed twice an hour each time. We took off shortly after dinner and didn't have any trouble getting into our formation. This target was supposed to be hit by our group alone and we finally ended up by not bombing it at all. We were briefed for visual bombing and then we got there over the target, a heavy overcast hung over the target area and made bombing impossible for us. Our fighter support was good and flak was heavy around target area, but not effective. We got back to our base and landed with a full bomb load. We still got credited for another mission.

MISSION

(21)

TARGET:	Mery sur Oise, France Flying Bomb Supply Depot
DATE:	Thursday August 3, 1944 – Plane #220-H
TAKE OFF:	13:31 5 hrs 26 mins.
LANDED:	18:57 oxygen
BRIEFED:	12:00 Bombs dropped at 17:07
BOMB LOAD:	8 – 1000 # Demolition Bombs
TARGET BOMBED:	23,800 ft – 30 below
	Our group had 36 planes

REMARKS:

We had our dinner at the usual time & returned to our hut shortly after over the PA system came the announcement that all crews were alerted, and to report to the briefing room. So we all got there around 12 o'clock and got all the information for the mission. We were the fifth ones to take off and didn't have any trouble getting into our formation at altitude. It was partly cloudy at the time and visibility was fairly good thru the mission. The channel was crowded with boats going back and forth with troop supplies. We flew on the very edge of our land troops over northern Normandy. I counted 13 landing strips that were already built on land taken from the Axis since D-Day. After flying about 30 mins. over enemy territory, bad weather set in and we were flying thru clouds at 24,000 ft…Putting up with this orders came over the air that everything was cancelled and everyone was supposed to turn back. Major Heaton was along with us and took it upon himself to continue on with this mission. After flying for a short time the clouds broke and we had good visibility for the bombing. This target took us completely around Paris out skirts and one could see it quite well. About two minutes before we dropped our bombs, the plane in front of us opened its bomb bay door and thru some carelessness by one of the crew members, an ammunition box dropped out the plane which knocked out the co-pilot's side window & front window. DeGood our co-pilot was hit on the left side and had to leave his post for first aid. Our pilot practically froze because of the cold wind that was coming thru this broken side. We finally dropped our bombs and then were anxious to get home in order to get DeGood to the doctor. Flak was heavy around the target and our plane suffered some hits. We broke away from the formation and flew a different course in order to save time and get DeGood to the hospital. The report and results of the bombing was excellent, and our group was complimented because we were the only ones that had bombed the target with such good results, after having all the others turned back.

* Gilmore gave him his mask and he also got hit in the back of the head. He gave DeGood first aid and he had to hold up a flak suit to the front window to keep the wind off of the pilot on the return trip home and he almost got blown out of the plane.

MISSION

(22)

TARGET:	Hamburg, Germany Oil Refinery
DATE:	Sunday August 6, 1944 Plane #118-V
TAKE OFF:	07:31 6 hrs. 33 mins.
LANDED:	14:04 Oxygen 4 ½ hrs.
BRIEFED:	04:00 Bombs dropped 12:00
BOMB LOAD:	12 – 500 # Demolition Bombs
TARGET BOMBED:	23,000 ft. – 25 below
	Our group had 30 Planes

REMARKS

We were awaken at 3 o'clock ate lunch. We took off as usual and hit a little prop wash on the way going up which isn't a very pleasant feeling. Our course took us over the North Sea which is a distance of 160 miles. Visibility was very good and we could see Denmark on the way, on our left as we headed for the target. We could see our target miles before. We half circled and came in for our bomb run. Everything was going fine until we opened up the bomb bay doors and only four minutes before bombs away, when our number two engine cut out this time and the number four engine also developed a run-away prop. It would have (been) suicide for us to continue on with our bombing under such circumstances, so the pilot gave the order to the navigator to drop our bombs, which he did immediately. This time the pilot feathered number two engine and then we only had power in the remaining three engines to get us back to our base. The flak was very heavy at the target and many planes suffered heavy damage.

Our Formation flew over the heart of Hamburg, because of the target. While we broke away from them and flew the outskirts in order to avoid being hit by Flak. Enemy Fighters were reported in this area and flying alone was not a very pleasant feeling. Our Fighters were around also, and we couldn't draw attention, to give us escort over enemy territory. We were over Germany for over an hour which isn't too bad. Visibility was good over Germany and we could see smoke and fire in several places all over Hamburg which indicated all targets were hit. We reached our base ahead of the others by 10 minutes or so & our Pilot buzzed the field because our Bombardier that flew with us on this mission completed his tour of duty 30 missions. The crew that shares the hut with us also completed their tour. After parking our plane and waited for transportation, when all of a sudden, we noticed two planes trying to land at the same time, one went head first into the ground & went up in flames. The second plane hit a short distance from the first and ended up with nothing left of the plane. All crew members of the first plane were lost and the second plane crew maybe left with only permanent injuries. Which is still a miracle happening for them to be alive.

― ― ― ― ― ― ― ―

MISSION

(23)

TARGET: Ostend, Belgium Oil Installations
DATE: Monday August 7, 1944 – Plane #258-N
TAKE OFF: 09:48   3 hrs. 13 minutes
LANDED: 13:01   Oxygen 2 hrs.

BRIEFED: 06:30
BOMB LOAD: 24-250 # Demolition Bombs
TARGET BOMBED: 22,000 Ft. 23 below
Our group had 12 planes

REMARKS

Just a few planes went out on this mission from our group because not many planes were available. The Hamburg raid crippled most of them, which was flown the day before. Visibility good at the time of take off except over the target and which made visual bombing impossible. We made two runs on the target and had to return back to our base with a full load of bombs. If this target had been in Germany we would have dropped our bombs on any secondary target of military importance. We saw a few of our Fighters around the target area and no flak for a change. This was our easiest mission so far and would like many more to complete our tour. Today's misson was the last one for the group and the entire group is breaking up and none of us know where we're heading from here. The main reason for breaking up is unknown and probably for the best, because the group had had tough luck ever since it started its operations the group losses have been around sixty full crews and many more planes which isn't a very good record for the short time it's been in operation. Our Group has been labeled "The Hard Luck Group" with most of the other 8th Air Force.

Only five crews finished their 30 missions tour with this group before breaking up. Only fourteen crews remain from seventy-two that originally started off with this group. Our group was in the Fourteenth Wing with the 44th and 392nd group 857th

Bomb Squadron 492nd Bomb Group. CREW 718 – HUT 16 and site one.

    Col. Snavley – Major Heaton   Our Group's Tail Marking

MISSION

(24)

TARGET:	Zwischenahn, Germany Airfield and Seaplane Base
DATE:	Tuesday August 15, 1944 Plane # 383-X
TAKE OFF:	09:09 4 hrs. 55 mins.
LANDED:	14:04 Oxygen 3 ½ hrs.
BRIEFED AT:	04:45 Bombs dropped 12:09
BOMB LOAD:	52-100 # Demolition Bombs
TARGET BOMB:	21,200 ft. – 16 below
	Our group had 21 planes

REMARKS

This was our first mission with this group, which was one of the easiest so far. The base itself is very convenient on most things and isn't half bad. We got into formation without any trouble and headed over the North Sea towards our target, visibility was good. The target was well hit, and was originally used for jet=propelled planes as well as a seaplane base. A large lake ajoins this field. Lake Awischenaher.

NOTES

August 23, 24 & 25th our crew spent a 28 hr pass in London. This was our third time we went to London on passes and had a grand time, this time without any disturbances from Flying Bombs.

MISSION
(25)

TARGET:	Cranienburg, Germany Air Field
DATE:	Sunday, August 27, 1944 Plane #340-3
TAKE OFF:	11:21 5 hrs. 18 mins.
LANDED:	07:45
BOMB LOAD:	20 – 250 # Demolition Bombs.
	Our group had 36 planes.

REMARKS

The weather wasn't too bad, although there was heavy ground fog, which was responsible for the late take off. We flew number three position in the lead element on this mission and were the first to land. We flew over the North Sea going to the target and hit bad weather just before the enemy coast. We hit some flak from the North Frisian islands. We flew around for awhile and finally got orders over the radio to return back to the base. The sky was just loaded with cumulus clouds which are always bad to fly through because of their terrific air current. The target we were supposed to hit was an Air Field which was only 16 miles north of Berlin. Our own Fighters were around us in great number.

MISSION

(26)

TARGET:	Karlsruhe, Germany Marshalling Fields
DATE:	Friday September 8, 1944 Plane #383-X
TAKE OFF:	07:22 8 hrs. 28 mins.
LANDED:	15:50 Oxygen 5 hrs.
BRIEFED AT:	04:15 Bombs dropped 11:56
BOMB LOAD:	5 – 1000 # Demolition Bombs
TARGET BOMBED:	24,000 ft. 40 below
	Our group had 30 planes

REMARKS:

The weather was just average and visibility at the time of take off was very poor. We were supposed to form at 8 thousand feet and had to go up to 16 thousand because of the clouds from ground up. We flew number three position in the lead element, which is always a good position to fly in. Visibility got very bad on the way to the target that we had to get up to 26 thousand feet in order to be out in the clear. The temperature at that altitude was 40 below, which is the coldest we ever hit so far. As we neared the target, visibility improved one hundred percent around the target area and we were able to bomb visual, which resulted in good bombing of the target. We had fairly good Fighter support and didn't see any enemy fighters. We hit flak around target area. After leaving the target one could see scores of targets well hit along our route back which took us all the way thru France.

MISSION
(26)

We flew close by Paris and one could see the famous Eiffel Tower. It wasn't so long ago that the places we flew over were in enemy[119] hands, which was a pleasant feeling not to expect flak. Karlsruhe is an important Rail Center for traffic supplying the Siegfried line, which was put out of commission a long time because of the number of bombers that hit this target (27 – 4 group squadrons). This was our longest mission so far and wasn't too bad considering that we were over enemy territory for only 40 minutes. Karlsruhe is located on the west of the Rhine River.

— — — — — — — —

MISSION
(27)

TARGET:	Ulm, Germany Marshalling Yards
DATE:	Sunday September 10, 1944
	Plane #247-H
TAKE OFF:	8 hrs. 18 mins.
LANDED:	14:41 Oxygen 6 hrs.
BRIEFED:	03:00 Bombs Dropped 11:16
BOMB LOAD:	20 – 250 # Demolition Bombs
TARGET BOMBED:	20,000 ft. 28 below
	Our group had 40 planes

---

119 This mission took place after the liberation of France by the Allied forces on August 25, 1944.

REMARKS

The weather was clear and it was still partly at the time we took off. We flew number 3 position in the high element on this mission. We were briefed to bomb an Oil Dump which was located a short distance out of Stuttgart and because of the overcast, it was necessary for us to bomb the secondary Target PFF, which was located in the same vicinity and also some on the way back without any damage to our plane. Fighter support was just average. We flew over the Seine, Rhine, Meuse, Moselle, Saar and the Danube River. After we left our target we flew near Stuttgart and saw it being blown up by other groups. We noticed other targets hit all along enemy territory on the way which indicated that the enemy is taking an awful beating. We didn't abort on any of our thirty missions, which is a excellent record.

702nd B. Sqdn. 445th B. Grp

Lt. Col Jones – Major Martin

De Good finished his tour on Set. 21st.
on a mission that took him to Coblenz. Germany.

— — — — — — — -

About the Author

Molly Brandenburg, Bud's daughter, is a writer, cartoonist, singer, actor and podcast host. As a child, Bud told Molly, "I want you to be a comedy singer," and his early belief in her creative gifts has been a continual source of inspiration for her.

Molly is the author and illustrator of two original books of cartoons, "Everyday Cat Excuses" and "The Truth About Cats." Her cartoons can also be seen on the global interior decorating website, www.Houzz.com. Molly also performs regularly on the Los Angeles nightclub scene (in top venues like The Viper Room) as lounge singer Miss Peggy Judy. She can also be heard regularly on Apple Podcasts as the host of the chart-topping Parcast Network podcasts, "Conspiracy Theories," "Unexplained Mysteries," and "Gone."

Muriel and Bud, young and in love during their engagement after the war.

Bud and his daughter Molly, aka lounge singer "Peggy Judy."

Molly Brandenburg, Bud's daughter.

THE END

www.ingramcontent.com/pod-product-compliance
Lightning Source LLC
Chambersburg PA
CBHW071939160426
43198CB00011B/1466